WORKING FOR PEANUTS

WORKING FOR PEANUTS

The Truly Heartwarming Story of
Project Linus

KAREN LOUCKS RINEDOLLAR

Editing: Donna Mazzitelli
Cover Design: Tina Taylor
Text Design: Andrea Costantine

Printed in the United States of America

First Edition
ISBN 978-0-615-49829-4

In loving memory, this book is dedicated to
Eddie Adams, Bob Rafferty, Jr. and Amara Wells.

CONTENTS

PROLOGUE

I received the call I'd been hoping for since the first days of Project Linus. It was from one of the Harpo producers at *Oprah*. They wanted an interview to see if I might be a good fit for Oprah's show. I was absolutely giddy sharing some of the heartrending stories experienced by Project Linus. A few weeks later, another call came with yet another interview. Interview by interview, we were working our way up the chain of command.

I had my eyes set on the brass ring—to be an actual guest on Oprah's show. Finally, I got the call! Yes, indeed, they wanted to feature Project Linus. This was the answer to our prayers and just in the nick of time. We were going to be saved! We'd be able to evolve as we'd envisioned, transporting Project Linus to the next stage of growth. Maybe we would have real office space instead of working from our kitchen tables. Maybe we could stop fretting about how to cover our ongoing expenses. Better yet, paid staff could finally be hired who would be able to turn the key at night, lock the doors behind them, and get on with their lives. At last, I could be compensated for my role at the helm of the Project Linus ship. What a much nicer vision than being plagued with this 24-7 need to catch up. Oh, the dreaming was divine!

There were two chairs set center stage. I entered from behind the stage and immediately zoomed in on Oprah seated in the left-hand chair facing the audience. I was so excited to finally meet her. Many an afternoon I'd laughed and cried with her through a variety of guests and topics. She's always exuded the feeling that she is everyone's girlfriend. Now, she and I were finally going to be face to face. I truly felt the anticipation of reuniting with a long-lost friend.

As I approached, Oprah stood and gave me a quick handshake. She motioned for me to have a seat. She gave me a smile and then seemed to mentally go somewhere else, preoccupied in her own thoughts. Complete silence enveloped us. The moment was surreal. Here I was, sitting in a chair opposite Oprah. Everything I'd dreamed of for Project Linus was coming to fruition. The years of devotion, dedication, hard work, and selfless giving to children in need by everyone involved with Project Linus were about to be rewarded. My heart swelled with joy and gratitude for this opportunity.

Introduction

I didn't invent the security blanket. Like Mrs. Fields of cookie fame, I simply discovered an effective way to market it. As a result, millions of people have been helped along the way. In my heart of hearts, I believe Project Linus was an answer to one of my prayers. I was used as a vessel to deliver a message to the world—a message of love, understanding, compassion and the notion that we all have the power to make a positive difference.

In late fall of 2010, as Project Linus was nearing its 15th anniversary, I experienced an overwhelming desire to put the Project Linus story down on paper. It is such a charming tale that people love to hear. Especially in these days of gloom and doom, with soothsayers falsely predicting that the end is near, the legend of Project Linus is an inspiring breath of fresh air.

As if on cue—and by sheer magic—those individuals appeared who would be instrumental in transforming this dream into a reality. I was invited to join a local writers group and found myself in the presence of many authors who were willing to share the lessons they had learned during their journeys. When asked when I wanted my book to be completed, I honestly answered, "Yesterday." A published author challenged me to write an outline by a certain date. I did it with relative ease.

With two weeks remaining in December, and winter's bleary weather upon us, I hunkered in front of my laptop accompanied by my goal to write the book before year's end. I wrote in airplanes. I wrote at my sister-in-law's beautiful bay front Clearwater, Florida home. I wrote in the car (as a passenger), and I wrote at our country home—a diminutive 1892 miner's cottage. I emailed the transcript, with one hour to spare, on New Year's Eve. I had literally lugged my briefcase around the tiny town, from party to party, until we reached the Over the Brim Inn—an adorable Westcliffe, Colorado Bed & Breakfast with WiFi. "Wow! I'm done!" So I thought.

This experience was similar to the time my husband and I redid our bathroom floor. Having never undertaken such an effort, I was a willing assistant and heeded to his expertise. In less than two hours, we removed the old carpeting and pad (yuck!), disconnected the toilet and pried off all the baseboards. Since the demolition seemed to take minutes, I felt as if the entire reconstruction was going to be a breeze.

We'd be done in no time at all! My husband just looked at me with the old "ignorance is bliss" gaze and smiled. The finished result was a beautifully patterned Travertine tile floor, but it took two weeks of patient measuring and careful laying of the pieces to achieve our masterpiece.

Such was the case with this book. I thought I was starting off the New Year with my book ready to roll. In January, the eye-catching cover was expertly pieced together by graphic artist Tina. She is a true pro, and after forty years of friendship, she knows what I like. It took her less than a week to create the perfect cover. Next, Dr. Laura Schlessinger responded promptly (and affirmatively) to my request that she write the foreword. Again—a piece of cake. But then, life seemed to get in the way.

First, one of my best friends, Tammy, lost her husband Bob and sister-in-law Amara to a horrific murder. Bob was a huge supporter of Project Linus and Amara was one of our finest quilters. How any of us made it through those first few weeks is a mystery. Even though some time has now passed since this tragic event, I'm still in denial that there can be such evil in the world and at such close range.

A few weeks after the murders, my mother had a stroke-like event. She was in the hospital in a rehab facility for six weeks. Trips back and forth to Virginia became part of my routine. My husband's mother was also struggling with late stages of Parkinson's disease. I can honestly say that, during those few months, the stress level in our lives was possibly the highest it has ever been. Being able to concentrate effectively on the book project just wasn't in the cards, and it was essentially shelved for awhile.

May marked a time of new beginnings. My stepdaughter

Kristen graduated with an engineering degree from the prestigious School of Mines and stepson Marcus graduated from Regis Jesuit High School. Such a time of celebration! Finally, the book was back on track, and I was once again making headway. I kept tweaking—adding new stories and more finishing touches—until finally someone wisely told me, "It's time to put down the pen."

I could tweak for the next five years and still not be done. It's not so much the verbiage but the stories that beckon. There are so many remarkable Project Linus tales to be told. Each time I get off the phone with another coordinator who has shared this voyage with me, I am filled with awe and wonder and reminded of even more people and events that took place over the past 15 years.

As much as I wish for every person and each experience to be included, I know it is time to set aside my pen and paper and release this book to the world. My hope is that the story of Project Linus inspires you as it has me.

Karen Loucks Rinedollar

CHAPTER
1

Finding My Holy Grail

How wonderful it is that nobody need wait a single moment before starting to improve the world.

- Anne Frank

Early mornings are always my favorite time of day. The house is quiet. The phone isn't ringing. My batteries are recharged. No one is putting demands on my schedule. It's all about me. With a clear head, it feels as if I can take on the world, like a ten-year-old child who wants to be an Olympic gold medal gymnast at the same time she desires to cure cancer—and wholeheartedly believes she can do both with relative ease.

On this particular morning, my lofty goal was to extricate myself from the bedroom without awaking any of the five slumbering dogs, two cats, husband or the horse groom who lived down the hall. A plastic-wrapped Sunday edition of the *Rocky Mountain News* lay waiting to be retrieved on the other side of our ten-acre ranch's front gates. Some goals are grande; others just seem that way at the time.

Being December in Colorado, my first hurdle was to bundle my body like the Michelin Man to keep from getting chilled to the bone during the few minutes I'd be outside. I made a quick stop at the kitchen on my way out to fire up the kettle. Bertha, a 70-pound silver Lercher (half Neapolitan mastiff and half greyhound—resembling a greyhound on steroids), stood groggily watching me from the hallway. Fortunately, she was the only one who picked me up on her radar. That was fine. She was my constant companion and wouldn't end up making noise or waking the rest of the household, thus keeping my sacred morning time intact.

A quick grab of a cozy coat off the rack, and I proceeded to slip quietly out into Colorado's deep freeze with Bertha by my side. Even the squeaking of the hinges on the wooden French doors didn't catch anyone else's attention. Frost carpeted the frozen dormant grass and dirt driveway. Bertha squatted daintily as she performed her morning piddle. A melted patch and steam arose marking her spot. With her long legs, she quickly resumed her favorite position—my shadow—as we approached the gate. It swung open easily, and there, just a few feet from the entrance, lay my morning's holy grail—the paper!

When we returned to the house, the water was just about to boil. I was able to reach it before the shrill whistle of the kettle could wake the sleeping brood. I made a cup of steaming hot tea, "miffed" it (English slang for "milk in first," versus the opposite "tiffed" for tea in first), then padded off to the living room. There, I assumed my favorite Sunday morning pose. Sitting on the floor, I opened the paper like a child eagerly unwrapping a Christmas present. Little did I know, one of the best presents I would ever receive lay under the periodical's plastic sleeve.

Being raised Presbyterian I wasn't someone who routinely spoke to a Higher Power with much ceremony. No prayer rugs facing east, no bended-knee time by the bed, no testimonies given in front of a congregation, not even grace at the dinner table. The closest I got to prayer as a child was the "Now I Lay Me" semi-nursery rhyme we said before sleep and the obligatory head bow during church service. When Sandy, a Jehovah's Witness neighbor, challenged me to start praying, I complied half-heartedly. It meant a lot to Sandy and wouldn't cost me a dime, so what the heck?

I quickly established a little ditty where I would pray for the health and safety of my family and friends, successful gigs for my husband and world peace. One can't forget world peace. Most significantly, I prayed for the inspiration to make a positive difference in the world. I was grateful for my life but was beginning to wonder, "Is this it?" The missing piece was not money or fame or any other "thing." I'd met a number of celebrities at this point and they certainly didn't seem any more content with their lot than Average Joe. What I yearned for was a divinely-inspired purpose—to be shown a way to contribute to making our world a better place. So far, my prayer had not been answered.

Although not typically obsessive-compulsive, I tend to

dissect the newspaper in a certain manner. Three stacks are quickly formed. One for the news, editorials, book reviews, and other items that require additional time devoted to reading. The second is for the immediate recyclables, usually the reams of advertisements and classifieds. The third is the fun pile, something I can fly through with relative ease—comics, money-saving coupons, the travel section and *Parade* magazine.

This morning, I started with *Parade* and flipped through the celebrity gossip section on the inside cover. Then, as if someone took my hand and moved the pages for me, I turned to the middle of the magazine. My excitement grew as I looked upon a two-page spread entitled, "Joy to the World," written by Pulitzer Prize winning photojournalist Eddie Adams. This was his Christmas gift to *Parade's* readership. He wrote of his thankfulness for his own son's health and his desire to share the stories of three children who were less fortunate. Eddie's photos were compelling. Each of these children showed spirit, bravery, and knowledge of a life of pain that no child should experience.

One picture in particular captivated me from the moment I laid eyes on it. It was of three-year-old Laura Williams. She was standing in a white-walled room, barefoot on light-colored carpeting. A slight tinge of pink imbued her diaphanous nightie; her head was covered with the downy fluff of a chemo patient. In her hand was a security blanket. She looked so innocent and ethereal, almost like a spirit who had already passed into the next realm. Laura stated, in her own three-year-old way, that the blanket had been lovingly made for her by an aunt. It helped Laura get through the rigors of cancer—the appointments, the treatments, the operations.

My immediate thought was how powerful a simple blanket could be with hopes, prayers and love hand-woven into it.

My mind churned. *What about the children who did not have someone to make one of these "magic" blankets for them?* After all, many people's lives are too busy to sit down and create a handmade gift. It is a far easier, quicker—and sometimes less expensive—option to go to the store and buy something that has been mass-produced. All of these questions and thoughts began to plant seeds in my heart, and even I could not have imagined the magnitude of what was about to take root.

I am a firm believer in the saying, 'there are no coincidences.' My head spun, as seemingly unrelated events from my life started to connect like a dot-to-dot drawing. It was as if the events were the series of dots that, up to now, couldn't quite connect, and this *Parade* article represented what was needed to complete the picture. Immediately, two distinct, recent events came to mind that suggested I might have an answer to the dilemma posed by my questioning.

CHAPTER
2

First Dive

*If I had to associate myself with one song, it would
probably be Let Love Rule. It's so simple and to the point.
It speaks for itself.*

- Lenny Kravitz

The first event occurred in January of that year. Peter
"Ginger" Baker, my husband at the time, was a
musician and a polo player. Together, we'd founded
the Mile High Polo Club in Parker the previous summer. We
coordinated polo matches at the club, followed by jazz every
Friday evening and Sunday afternoon. Vehicles were charged
$10, whether an RV with 20 people in it or a single rider on a
motorcycle. One hundred percent of those funds were divided
and donated to Dreampower Animal Rescue and Adoption
Alliance.

These events were such a success that we decided to try
our hand at a much grander affair. This time, all the funds

would be donated to the Rocky Mountain Children's Cancer Center. To maximize the profits for the children, we worked closely with people who were supposed to be experienced fundraisers. We held a polo and jazz extravaganza in conjunction with one of Denver's largest annual events—the Great Western Stock Show. Lavish parties took place, and elite players flew in from Hawaii and Chicago.

The event itself ended up reminding me of a Christmas card we once received from Eric Clapton's manager, Roger Forrester. On the cover was a drawing of Eric and Roger sitting in a dilapidated old van. It had flattened tires, dangling side mirrors, rust spots, damaged fenders and broken windows. The side of the van read "EC Blues Tour." When the card was opened, there was a whole string of posh vans following the "beater," identified as being for EC Wardrobe, EC Hair Stylist, EC Security, EC Caterers, EC Guitar Strings, EC Riggers, EC Lights, EC Sound, EC Video, and EC Techs. On and on it went. The saying on the inside of the card was "The Management would like to quell recent press rumors that there is any money to be made out of the blues. Merry Christmas!"

Much to my chagrin—and despite all the monies collected at this event—very little made its way to the actual charity. It seemed there was a line of vendors a mile long with their hands out waiting to be paid—caterers, the venue site, printers, airlines and a whole string of other miscellaneous charges. Despite our noble intentions, the event ended up only making a few thousand dollars for the charity. I was extremely disheartened.

At a party, during the summer following the event, I had some quality face-time with the director of the cancer center,

Dr. Edward Arrenson. I apologized profusely for not being able to raise more funds, and he stated that this scenario often represented the outcome to a fundraiser. Unless there are actual sponsors for the event, after all the bills are paid, the charities typically receive a small portion of the funds collected. This didn't sit well with me at all.

The second synchronous event I recalled that morning of Christmas Eve was the fact that I'd recently learned how to crochet and I'd become addicted to the activity. I'd always been passionate about needlecrafts. I'd spend many an hour doing needlepoint and cross stitching in college. It was a form of relaxation- a way of getting away from the stresses of daily dorm life. From a remarkably young age, I'd been a knitter, thanks to Mom's patient teachings. I eagerly watched her make knitted cough pillows for patients who recently had their chests opened for heart surgery. I was able to employ my voracious energy and whip up boxes of yarn squares throughout my childhood.

Mom used to say that knitting was far more refined than crocheting. "Nice girls learn how to knit," she told me. This logic was a classic Mom-ism- one of those things that make you go "huh?" Similar to, "If Cher would just cut her hair, she would gain some weight." First, I do not think Cher was interested in putting on weight. Second, I think Cher loved her long hair—it was part of what made her "Cher," at least in her early career. Needless to say, I didn't learn how to crochet until I was 32.

I was part of a Masters swim team in Castle Rock. One day between sets, I overheard two of my teammates, Shirley

Hardin and Donna Ryman, talking across the lane lines about getting together for The Hookers Club. Knowing Shirley and Donna, I found this hilarious. Both were over 50 at the time, highly responsible citizens, and the last thing I would ever consider either of them was a Hooker. I soon discovered they were humorously referring to themselves as being crocheters, not prostitutes, since crocheters use a hook type instrument to weave their precious yarn together.

I asked if I could attend one of their get-togethers, and they warmly welcomed me into their group of around a half dozen ladies who had known each other for decades. Several of them patiently took the time and offered encouragement as I learned the fundamentals of crocheting—first chaining, then single crocheting, then double crocheting. Soon, I made my first item, a scarf, and I was "hooked." I couldn't stop. Scarves turned into blankets, and I was soon blanketing my friends and family. To this day, my mother keeps the blue-green, basic, double-crochet blanket—one of my first—on the back of her couch.

I am a kinesthetic learner, which means I learn best when in motion—through physical interaction—as opposed to the way most other adults learn through visual or auditory means. As a child, it was pure torture to be told to sit still, which is what one is required to do in a school or church situation. Although never officially diagnosed, I'm sure that a diagnosis of ADHD wouldn't be far off the mark.

A study was published a 2003 issue in the American Journal of Occupational Therapy showing that children with ADHD, if allowed to sit on a therapy ball instead of a classic chair, have improved behavior and were able to sit still, focus and write words more clearly. In 2007, Rochester's

Mayo Clinic also found that there were benefits to classrooms without chairs. The big bouncing balls as seen in gyms make for excellent "chairs" as it take core muscles to keep the balls from moving- therefore, although not seemingly in motion, the person sitting on the ball is doing quiet, un-interruptive exercising. Mayo found that by being able to move around more, student actually become more attentive. I suspect that the same benefits may be found by people who doodle, twist a pencil, wiggle a foot or even in my case- crochet. Retention seems to increase tremendously.

I've used this trick many times when full attention was a mandate, including when I attended fire academy to become a State Certified Firefighter and EMT (Emergency Medical Tech). I made a deal with my instructors that I could crochet during class and sit in the back of the room so as not to be distracting to others. My ability to absorb the information while in motion guaranteed I'd get an excellent grade. It worked!

Crocheting was the perfect anecdote for my need to move. It wasn't long before I was dubbed a "Turbo Crocheter." I could whip out a baby blanket during the four-hour flight back to my home state of Virginia while watching a movie and having a conversation with the person next to me. The repetitive motion in crocheting makes being able to do it while not looking a breeze and if there ever is a mistake, with only one stitch on the hook, it's much easier to correct than knitting. Within months, I'd made over a half-dozen blankets and wanted to keep applying my newly-learned skill. There were so many color combos to play with, and so many stitches to learn!

Over the years, I've met many others with a similar

compulsion. Maybe it's the repetitive motion that is addictive. Perhaps it's the power of creating. Researchers at the Mind-Body Medical Institute at Harvard Medical School discovered that knitting, crocheting and embroidery are as effective as meditation, yoga or chanting in triggering the body's relaxation response. Apparently, the repetitive motions block the hormone noradrenalin. That, in turn, lowers blood pressure and heart rate, leaving one feeling more peaceful. In one study, needle workers' heart rates dropped by 11 beats per minute while they worked! Whatever induced this obsession, it is partly what fueled me to want to give back to the children.

One challenge avid crafters face early on is that there are *only* so many family members and friends interested in receiving their handiwork. If crafters are prolific in their hobby, they quickly run out of recipients. I correctly guessed that there were many crafters who would be thrilled to donate their needlework, especially when it helped a child.

So there I was, on a Sunday morning, reading the paper—like every other Sunday throughout the year—except on this particular day, the pieces of my passions were coming together, quite unexpectedly. When I thought of the children who could use an extra emotional and physical boost by receiving a handmade blanket of their own, as well as my recent experiences with the Rocky Mountain Children's Cancer Center and The Hookers, it was as if all the planets came into alignment. My prayers to discover a way to make a difference in the world were being answered!

CHAPTER
3

Something to Hold Onto

*Don't judge each day by the harvest you
reap but by the seeds that you plant.*

- Robert Louis Stevenson

By this time, sounds of life emanated from around the house. I nearly sprinted back to the bedroom, accompanied by my buddy Bertha. I gently pushed some of the slumbering dogs out of the way as I climbed onto the bed. In a gush, the words came pouring out as I explained my plan to Ginger. I was going to make blankets for kids at the Rocky Mountain Children's Cancer Center, and 100% of my efforts would be received by the kids! I would make a difference in the lives of these children by giving them something to hold on to, literally and figuratively.

Ginger, with uncharacteristic optimism, thought this was a brilliant idea and gave his seal of approval to my enthusiastic proposal. I think it helped that his own mother, Ruby, was an avid fiber artist. Rarely, was she seen without being in the midst of some kind of sweater or decorative piece on her ever-moving knitting or embroidery needles. She was constantly doing things for others. As Ginger took a moment to digest the situation, he stretched and casually asked if there was any hot tea. Priorities!

Since it was Christmas Eve and the weekend, I had to wait a couple of days to contact the Rocky Mountain Children's Cancer Center and schedule an appointment with Dr. Edward Arrenson. I felt strongly that I needed to run this idea by him. After all, what better sounding board than someone on the front lines? Fortunately, I was able to meet with him quickly. I've never been exceptionally patient, so in the days leading up to our meeting, I crocheted a half-dozen sample blankets. I wanted to be able to present a variety of sizes, colors and patterns, since I knew kids come in a wide variety of shapes and personalities. One size definitely does not fit all.

As I sat crocheting, each new row added to the foundation of this idea and the strength of my feelings. To meld experiences and talents and simultaneously help others in need just felt like the right thing to do. Experimenting with different colors and pattern combos felt a bit like playing a mad scientist in a lab. If I could just come up with the right combination, perhaps it would be enough to tip the scale for a patient. If the saying "Attitude is everything" is true, perhaps receiving a handmade blanket could be a tipping point for that patient. Knowing that a complete stranger cared about their welfare, may give a patient that slight edge that they need to get through their ordeal. My confidence level multiplied in direct proportion to the increasing number of blankets.

⌒‿

With eager anticipation and arms laden with freshly-made blankets, I rode the elevator up to the third floor of the medical center. Just as I remembered him from our previous meetings, Ed was warm and welcoming. When I pitched the idea of giving blankets to his patients, he responded immediately with his naturally positive gusto. He embraced the idea that patients could benefit from treatment and tools beyond traditional, Western medical methods. Ed called his nurses in and let me pitch the idea to them. They loved it.

The next sales job was going to be the most nerve-racking of all, or so I thought. Ed led me, with the blankets, out to several patients who were receiving infusions. Despite probably not feeling particularly well, and certainly appearing as if they had seen better days, they took to the blankets like ducks to water. No instructions needed! Oddly, it seemed that I'd brought just the right number, and they were perfect sizes for the children who were there. Naturally, I did not want to give a baby blanket to a teen or overwhelm a toddler with a blanket too large.

As I was leaving the office, I asked Ed how many patients he worked with in a year. His estimate was somewhere around one hundred. Classic Karen style, I immediately opened mouth, inserted foot, and set a verbal goal to "blanket" each of the children at the Rocky Mountain Children's Cancer Center in 1996. Despite being considered the "Turbo Crocheter," a hundred is still a lot of blankets for one person to make. Being an active individual, the sedentary lifestyle required to reach this lofty goal single-handedly, would be a mind and body breaker for me. I was going to need help!

Given that Parker is about a 40-minute drive from Denver, I could not just sit still behind the steering wheel as I drove home. My mind was going at warp speed. I had to share this news with someone who would listen with an open mind. Tina Taylor has been one of my best friends since we met back in fourth grade. Believe me, over the decades Tina has heard her fair share of enthusiastic calls on the latest, greatest scheme traversing its way across my brain cells. As I pitched the idea to her of starting a community effort to blanket the pediatric cancer patients, instead of throwing cold water over my eagerness, she asked one straightforward question, "What are you going to call it?" I think she had a hunch that this might be something monumental, and it would indeed need its own name.

CHAPTER 4

All Aboard!

The time to hesitate is through.

- Jim Morrison

Project Blankie was the first idea that made its way across my lips, and I immediately tried to suck it back in like a breath of cold air on a chilly winter's morning. "Rewind! Forget I ever said that," I quickly said to Tina. This name sounded pathetic, wimpy *and* uninspiring! The image of Charlie Brown's best buddy quickly came to mind, and Project Linus immediately replaced Project Blankie.

I wanted this venture to be fabulous, so why not tap into an already popular figure known worldwide for his close relationship with his security blanket—the loveable, highly intelligent, Linus?! However, I wasn't sure about the legalities of using such a famous character and knew there were licensing agreements that would have to be considered.

As I began this journey, one of the first letters to leave my home was to United Media. They were the newspaper syndication service that ran the Peanuts comic strip. It was essential that they know of my intention to use Project Linus as the name of this charity and to adopt the image of Linus as our mascot. I was thrilled at the possibility of receiving Charles Schulz's personal seal of approval. If I was going to ask, why not ask "big"!?! Plus, if they were going to put the legal kibosh on this idea, it would be best to find out early in the game.

The Hooker's Club soon had another of their meetings, and I pitched the fledgling idea of Project Linus to them. They met the concept with immediate enthusiasm. Shirley Hardin was just putting the finishing touches on a crocheted blanket and generously presented it to me as the first official donation! That was one down and ninety-nine to go to reach my goal of 100 for the Rocky Mountain Children's Cancer Center patients! The following week, she donated another, as did other members of the Hooker's Club. Project Linus was on a roll!

January 1996 ensued with a flurry of activity. There was a lot that needed to fall into place, so I did what any respectable journalism major would do—I contacted the media. I was sure there were many people in the Parker community who would love to make a blanket for these children. Who could resist doing something for a child with cancer? I could not, and I was sure not many other people could either.

I contacted Jim Kelly, who wrote a column called Highway

83 for the local newspaper, named after the road that bisects the town of Parker. His column consisted of the local goings-on. Jim's office was located directly above the art framing/ coffee shop where I occasionally worked, and he often stopped in for a cup of coffee. He seemed to have a heart of gold, and when I pitched Project Linus to him—kaboom—it appeared in the next week's paper. He even did a follow-up the subsequent week, because there had been such a positive response from the community. Knitters, crocheters and quilters were all revving up their needlecraft skills and working on blankets for the kids at the Rocky Mountain Children's Cancer Center.

Ever the optimist, I decided it was time to let the big dogs know about Project Linus. Hovering over the computer like a hungry hawk watching a mouse-laden field, I cranked out dozens of letters to everyone all the way from Oprah on down. Anyone who had a television show—national or local—was fair game, from *Good Morning America* to *Hello Denver* to local cable *DC Channel 8*. Undoubtedly, there were viewers who would be interested in joining us. Whether young moms chasing after rugrats, or retirees, or people home sick from work, there were lots of people out in "TV Land" wanting to make a difference, and Project Linus was the path that could take them there. I knew from experience that Project Linus was an item of significant value that the stations could provide to their viewers and they should be excited to include the effort in their programming!

I contacted celebrities of every genre and asked if they would help Project Linus continue its endeavors and make a blanket that could be used for a fundraiser. Already, I was seeing rolls of stamps and reams of paper being utilized, so it seemed only a matter of time before some kind of fundraising would be needed.

Within a month my routine walk to the mailbox brought a lovely surprise. The brown-paper exterior of the box did not reveal any of the excitement that was about to take Project Linus on an evolutionary step forward. Vanna White, the *Wheel of Fortune* letter-turner extraordinaire, responded to one of my many missives. She sent a beautifully crocheted pink baby blanket and wished me all the best with this endeavor. Someone outside of Parker, with the added bonus of having celebrity status, had actually taken notice of the Project Linus effort and provided encouragement that said this was the right thing to do! I felt like delivering a celebratory shout of "All aboard! The Project Linus train is getting ready to pull out of the station!" That small box delivered a huge shot of encouragement and the impetus I needed to continue forward full steam ahead. As is said, just ask and ye shall receive.

From the moment the batch of letters for show producers hit the outgoing mail, it was as if someone turned my life into overdrive. The sporadic hurry-up-and-wait pace of life as a volunteer firefighter and wife of a musician turned into a vortex of activity. A wise person once said, "Don't confuse activity with results." The Project Linus effort however was evolving by leaps and bounds. Each of the efforts, no matter how random and crazy, seemed to thrust the momentum forward.

The book, *The Secret*, talks about putting our intentions out to the Universe and watching miracles work to help us reach our goals by using the Law of Attraction. It's as if the Universe can't help itself. This is exactly what began to happen with Project Linus. It truly felt as if any time Project Linus encountered a hurdle, the Universe whispered answers in my ear and the obstacle vanished. The right person would show up or the next piece of the puzzle revealed itself. This happened over and over again.

One of the most important lessons that an EMT learns is to *document, document, document*. This rule was easily applied to Project Linus. The initial thought was simply to keep organized in order to send out handwritten thank you notes. At an early age, my mother instilled the importance of sending a well-constructed and sincere note to someone who took the time to do something for me. She used to say that it would take far less time to write a thank you note to my grandmother or aunt than it took them to go shopping, pick out a gift, wrap it and send it to me. In the infinite wisdom of a preteen, I felt it was a pointless exercise constructed to cause me great angst.

Of course, my mother was right. Much has been said, especially recently, about the power of the handwritten note, probably because it is such a rare occurrence to receive one of these gems. There are even companies now that send out cards meant to look like a handwritten note.

The first President Bush was a full-fledged believer in handwritten notes. Supposedly, he attributed his successful political career to this habit. Every morning, he would have his assistant lay out thank you notes. He'd then write a few lines to people he had met the previous day. Perhaps it was the flight attendant who delivered his coffee with a smile, or a librarian who personally helped him find a book, or even the trash man who set his empty bins neatly on the side of his driveway after they'd been emptied. When it came time to run for office, these people remembered the warm note they received from Mr. Bush and often rewarded him with their vote.

A plain steno pad was the first of my many notebooks. It started with a trickle of entries. Soon, that trickle became a meandering stream and ultimately, a fast-moving river. As readers from the Parker newspaper articles began to hear about Project Linus, the notepad expanded exponentially. It was like the old Faberge Organic shampoo commercials—someone participated in Project Linus, then they told two friends, and they told two friends, and so on, and so on and so on.

CHAPTER
5

Children's Crusade

*One of the best gifts for someone who's 'on the mend' is
a knitted or crocheted afphan. Just imagine snugggling
into a soft blanket, knowing that every stitch was made by
someone who cares about the challenges you're facing!*

- Vanna White

The blanket donations started with individuals, and church groups soon followed. Early on, I received a call from someone in the Relief Society at a local L.D.S. church (The Church of Jesus Christ of Latter Day Saints, a.k.a. the Mormon Church). They said they were holding a meeting Valentine's night and would like me join them. They wanted me to explain where the blankets would go that they'd be making that night. Ginger rarely celebrated holidays, so spending that evening at a church with blanket makers sounded like an exciting idea. Everyone was so kind and welcoming, and at the end of the night, I left with four blankets. It may not have been the most romantic of

Valentine's nights, but it was definitely filled with heartfelt kindness.

January 1996			
Shirley Hardin	Castle Rock, CO	2 crocheted blankets	1 light green, 1 multicolored
Jane Brown	Castle Rock, CO	Quilted baby blankets	
Marge Durand	Parker, CO	17 Quilts	
Karen Loucks	Parker, CO	2 crocheted blankets	1 yellow, 1 wine

February 1996			
Vanna White	Hollywood, CA	1 crocheted	pink
Jane Brown	Castle Rock, CO	1 crocheted	pink
Marge Durand	Parker, CO	23 quilts	
Karen Loucks	Parker, CO	3 crocheted	1 yellow, 1 patriotic, 1 teal
Mormon Church	Parker, CO	4 tied quilts	
Trinity Lutheran Church	Parker, CO	11 quilts	
Carri Sambrano	Elizabeth, CO	7 quilts and blankets	
Sandy & Kara Schaub	Parker, CO	1 quilt with stuffed envelope pockets	

A subsequent call came from the L.D.S. church. Another group, the Ponderosa Young Women, was making blankets and wanted to know if I could come by. SURE! This time, I was given over a dozen blankets. Then, I received another call from the L.D.S. The Parker Relief Society asked me to stop by. This was a different Relief Society. I quickly learned about the L.D.S. church structure. It seemed that each of the Relief Societies belonged to a Ward (congregation). The different Wards then came together to form a Stake. Very early on, Project Linus was the lucky recipient of a bounty of blankets from the Parker Stake. Other local churches started to participate, and word about Project Linus began to spread like wildfire.

The Internet was rapidly growing. I was an early user of AOL and found it to be an incredibly helpful tool. There were chat rooms where I could meet other knitters, crocheters and quilters from around the country and the world. One of the first outside supporters of Project Linus was a wonderful gal from Pennsylvania. Her name was Carol Tornetta, and she joined our ranks very early on. Not only was she bright, but she also had a great sense of humor. As a mother of two and an active volunteer in the school system, Carol understood the power of people helping others in need. She was to be a crocheter, and quickly started to spread the word around her corner of Pennsylvania. It felt so exciting to have a complete stranger from halfway across the country run with this idea.

With blankets and volunteers rolling in, I soon realized the blanket makers needed a name for themselves. The name "blanket donor," always sounded a bit cold to me. It seemed like our contributors should be called something as warm and fuzzy as the product they were so generously creating. The name "Blanketeer" joined the lexicon of Project Linus, referring to anyone who makes a blanket for the effort. It was the combination of Blanket and Volunteer and sounder a little more exciting than Blanketer. It was also a witty twist on the famous name Mouseketeer—members of the Mickey Mouse Club, like Annette Funicello, Justin Timberlake, Christina Aguillera and Britney Spears. The name felt fun, playful and child-friendly. To the best of my knowledge, Carol Tornetta, gets credit for this clever moniker

⌒⌒

Around the end of February, I received a phone call from a producer of ABC's *Mike and Maty* show asking if I would be available to fly to L.A. the first week of March and appear on their show. "OH, YEAH! Just try stopping me!" This again was in response to one of the many letters I'd sent. I knew that just throwing empty hooks into the water was not enough to entice a fish, but once properly baited, those producers couldn't resist!

Before jetting off to L.A., however, I had an extremely important mission to accomplish. Between the individuals who responded to the local press and the various churches' generosity, Project Linus was quickly approaching my 100-blanket goal. I had already delivered a few dozen blankets to the Rocky Mountain Children's Cancer Center accompanied by some incredibly eager Blanketeers, including quilter-extraordinaire Marge Durand and her immensely good-natured husband, Ad. They were such a fun couple— retirees with soft hearts for children, a keen eye for quilt design and a flashy Corvette to boot! Any time I received a special request for a blanket, I knew that Marge could fill the bill. This happened a few times, like when Marge learned that one of the young patients was from Nebraska. Being a Nebraskan herself, she immediately whipped up a beautiful red-and-white quilt that could have been a contender in any quilt show. And she had never even met the child!

It was now time to deliver the remainder of the hundred-blanket goal. About a dozen excited Blanketeers, including

Marge and Ad, joined me on this momentous delivery. Dr. Arrenson's nurse led us to a conference room with a long table. She asked us to lay our bounty of blankets on the table and also requested that we set aside a few blankets for some of the pediatric cancer patients who were in nearby Presbyterian St. Luke's Hospital. At that time, we did not know the name or age of the patients, so we put aside a few neutrally-themed, unisex blankets.

The remaining blankets were piled across the conference room table, and each child was then given the opportunity to walk around and unhurriedly pick out his or her blanket. All of us beamed through tear-filled eyes as we witnessed the children in their selection process. Children who had every right, in my opinion, to be selfish and angry, were instead, so extremely sweet, so gentle, so appreciative, and so mature.

One child in particular captured my heart. He had just finished receiving a spinal tap. Previously, I'd seen a video of someone receiving this procedure, and it was no walk in the park. In fact, it looked like downright torture. Dr. Arrenson knew all the kiddos' names and asked the boy how the tap had gone. The patient shrugged his shoulders and acted as if it was no big deal. He paced around the table and spotted the blankets we'd set aside. One was a blue fleece blanket with images of Porky Pig on it. I was struck by the likeness this child had with Porky; a soft tuft of hair, bloated body and face, and pink—extremely pink—skin. He immediately seemed to relate to the Porky blanket, and when he reached for it, someone mentioned that we'd put it aside for a patient at the nearby hospital.

"ARE YOU KIDDING ME?" I thought. It was a random blanket, and this child wanted it. The potential hospital recipient didn't even know he was going to receive a blanket, let alone one with a specific cartoon character on it. The boy's father was remarkably tender as he explained to his son that this blanket was going to another child. Without a grumble, the boy gently returned "Porky" to his spot and pivoted back toward the conference table to pick out his second choice.

I practically hurdled myself over the table to get to the Porky blanket. "Please, take the blanket. It would be an honor for us to give you this blanket," I said. The child so unselfishly responded, "It's okay. I know it's for someone else." "No!" I insisted, "The recipient has no idea what will be on his blanket. We can pick out another beautiful blanket for him." The boy beamed as he reached out for it. He then hugged his Porky blanket in an embrace similar to pictures I've seen of returning Vietnam Vets reuniting with their families. This was his new source of comfort; the solace it brought this young boy seemed to enwrap his father as well. A blanket's ability to provide consolation to both children and their parents was nothing short of magical!

This boy was truly endearing. I had many friends with young children and witnessed the temper tantrums that can occur at that age. Full-blown dramatics in grocery store aisles, meltdowns at the zoo, and even the nonchalance of ripping through mountains of birthday presents certainly led me to wonder about the destiny of this modern generation. This little boy however—who had all the right in the world to be on edge from the physical and mental torment he'd endured—was mature, calm, cool, and collected. After witnessing the way he gracefully handled the potential of not getting what he wanted, my faith was restored. Out of the mouths of babes, indeed!

As I left the center that day, I said goodbye to the magnificent folks I carpooled with. They were heading back to Parker. I was going to the airport to catch my flight to Los Angeles and be on a national television show!

CHAPTER 6

Star Treatment

Love and compassion are necessities, not luxuries.
Without them humanity cannot survive.

- Dalai Lama

The flight from Denver to L.A. is relatively short, approximately 2 hours and 15 minutes. It's just enough time to take a rejuvenating nap, complete the Sudoku & crossword puzzles in the in-flight magazine, have the battery of my laptop die, or encounter a terrifically intriguing person.

Life stories have mesmerized me ever since I was an elementary school student who practically inhaled a biography a night. Usually, it was about an historical figure like Betsy Ross, Benjamin Franklin, Eleanor Roosevelt, P.T. Barnum, or Babe Ruth. As long as it was biographical, it didn't matter much who it was about. These stories were all so interesting, and I felt almost like a Peeping Tom peering into another's life. In addition to books, the Biography Channel and historical documentaries produced by Ken Burns are some of my favorite programs.

A stimulating conversation on an airplane can invoke the same level of fascination for me. I have always dreamed of writing a book of "ordinary people" biographies, since these everyday Joe's (and JoAnne's) are often more fascinating than the lifestyles of the rich and famous. There are so many heroes in our midst whose chivalrous actions never see the light of day. Never win an Oscar, a Pulitzer Prize, or receive a dinner invitation to the White House from the President. No Hollywood movie contracts. Yet they keep plodding along, making this world a better place without any heraldry or financial reward.

The March 2nd flight to L.A. for the taping of ABC's *Mike and Maty* show provided me with yet another message confirming that Project Linus was on the right path. From my bird's-eye-view window seat, I struck up a conversation with the "church lady" wedged in the middle seat next to me. Aside from looking visibly uncomfortable in the constricted seating, she seemed to be perfectly at ease with the world around her. Malia was her name—the same first name as an old schoolmate from Oakridge Elementary School. Her attitude was all sunshine and roses, and she was going on her first trip to California to assist her sister with a mission trip to Mexico.

When Malia switched topics and asked me about my trip, it was one of my first opportunities to use my Project Linus elevator speech on a complete stranger. I was a bit nervous to share my reason for going. What if Malia thought Project

Linus was a silly idea? What if she thought the viewers wouldn't find it a compelling topic? What if she started pushing buttons that would make me nervous about going on a national television show?

Any cause for anxiety seemed for naught. Malia instantly became Project Linus' newest cheerleader. I soon discovered that when Malia was about to pick up her new daughter for adoption in South Korea, some of her girlfriends threw her a baby shower. One of the treasured gifts she received was a hand-knitted pink-and-white blanket. It was compact enough to fit into her suitcase, so it was one of the few things she brought along when she and her husband flew overseas to meet their new daughter.

The little girl was a year old and had been living with a foster family. She had developed a strong bond with her foster mother. When it was time for her to go with her new family, the little girl and foster mom were both distraught. Once Malia and her husband took her back to the hotel, the little girl cried hour after hour all the way through the first night. No amount of singing, cooing, hugs or consoling would calm the child.

The next morning, after a sleepless night and feeling like a failure as a mother, Malia remembered she'd brought the blanket with her. When she wrapped her daughter with it, the little girl immediately quieted down. She seemed to love the pink color and softness of the blanket. For the first time, she allowed herself to be calmly held, and she promptly fell asleep in her new mother's arms. Malia told me that the child is now twelve years old and still treasures her blanket. Malia knew firsthand the magic that a handmade security blanket could perform. I got off the plane that day in awe of Malia's story and felt even more assured that Project Linus was on the right track.

⌒〰

ABC can be credited with the VIP treatment I received, starting with my arrival at the Los Angeles airport. A white-gloved, uniformed driver was waiting in the baggage area with my name written on a placard. A stretch limo chauffeured me to the historic Roosevelt Hotel in downtown Hollywood, where a beautiful suite adorned with a teeming fruit-and-wine basket heralded my arrival. I couldn't help but reflect on how things had suddenly changed in my life. I used to travel around the world as personal manager to my celebrity husband. Now, I was the one being wined and dined!

As a firm believer of mixing business with pleasure, I had the delight of dining with one of my best friends, Ken, that evening on Melrose Avenue, and we later dropped by to visit my ole L.A. roommate and high school classmate, Brenda, who had recently given birth to a beautiful baby boy. How wonderfully meaningful it was to reconnect with some of the significant people in my life, especially as I launched into this next phase of my life's journey! Everyone surrounding me became a piece of my blanket of courage, strength, and confidence.

The following morning, Nancy, one of my girlfriends from Santa Barbara, met me at the hotel for breakfast. We used to live near each other, and she was my favorite massage therapist. It was a fantastic opportunity to catch up and be tended by her calm presence. On the room service menu was an intriguing selection called the Japanese Breakfast. What an indulgence it turned out to be—hot tea along with delicious veggies, soup, tofu, and fruit!

The limo arrived promptly at the appointed time and delivered both Nancy and me to the ABC studio where taping of the *Mike and Maty* show took place. We were whisked to a spacious dressing room. Mike—one of the show's hosts—dropped by for a quick visit with a warm greeting to make us feel welcome. Although this may seem like a common courtesy for a show host to do, it doesn't always happen. That small bit of effort on Mike's part helped ensure my comfort level and made for a more relaxed segment.

I was then taken to the makeup room. I'd experienced these types of rooms before when I used to do extra work on movies. This time however they planned to enhance what I looked like, instead of trying to make me look like an image of someone else. I'd learned previously that the makeup artist chair can be an excellent source of beauty tips, and I was excited for "today's lesson." I soon found out that Blistex, which at the time was a popular lip product amongst my peers, should be used to dry out cold sores, not as a lip moisturizer. No wonder my lips always felt parched!

As I received the glamour treatment, the makeup artist excitedly shared with me that Eddie Adams was also appearing on the show. Assuming Eddie was some star from one of the current popular shows, I told her I didn't know who he was, because I rarely watched television. She was shocked to learn we hadn't owned a television in years. It turned out that Eddie was the man who took the photos and wrote the *Parade* article that inspired me to start Project Linus. Wow! What a fantastic opportunity to thank this gentleman! Here was one more serendipitous event! Little by little, pieces just kept coming together.

After makeup, came the hair stylist. She was a true professional and worked wonders on my fair mane. She also seemed extremely excited that Eddie Adams would be there. I started to visualize what this journalist looked like. The image of a 40-something Clark Kent—pencil-neck geek with thick spectacles—came immediately to mind. So much for my psychic powers and imagination, as I could not have been more wrong!

The cameras were on "break for commercial placement," and Mike and Maty welcomed me to join them in a comfortable chair next to their couch. We had a friendly chat for a few minutes and I was put at complete ease. Finally, it was time for me to be introduced.

Lights! Camera! Action!

The cameras began to roll, and there I was, being taped for a national television show. They asked me wonderfully leading questions that helped make for an informative and heartwarming exchange. It was my hope that some viewers would be inspired to send blankets to expand the blanketing efforts to other hospitals, now that we'd reached our Rocky Mountain Children's Cancer Center goal. After a few minutes of chatting about Project Linus, they broke for another commercial with promises that Eddie Adams would join us for the next segment.

I was so excited that I would get to thank this kind soul for his inspiration. Finally, the intro music started up again, and they announced Eddie's name. A mysterious gentleman donning a black Fedora and black coat shuffled across the stage and plunked down next to me on the guest couch. His silver hair was pulled back into a ponytail, and he wore celebrity sunglasses. As Mike and Maty interviewed Eddie,

I listened in awe. This man was a hero. He had shot photos of five wars, won a Pulitzer Prize, and had Presidents and celebrities sit for him on a regular basis. Despite all these worldly experiences, Eddie's piercing blue eyes softened and tears welled up, as he spoke of the children from his *Parade* article. He stated that he was thrilled his work had inspired an effort to assist children.

By the time we broke for commercial, Eddie and I had bonded. I was honored that this truly remarkable person wrote the article which inspired Project Linus. It felt strange that I never even considered the writer behind the article until today—especially since I was a journalist myself! I felt compelled to share with him that he did not look anything like the pencil-neck geek I imagined. To my surprise, Eddie confided that he thought I'd be a plump, Midwestern lady in a polka-dot dress. We exchanged contact info and promised to keep in touch.

Soon after, a limo swished its way through the heavy L.A. traffic, returning Nancy and me back to the Roosevelt. We said our goodbyes, and she returned to Santa Barbara. Another friend, Joanie, who lived in the neighborhood joined me for lunch. She was thrilled to hear about the studio experience and prophetically stated that Project Linus was going to make a difference in the lives of many, many children. When she departed, I was left to dream alone about the possibilities that lay ahead.

On my way back to Denver later that afternoon, I stared at the view from my window seat. Unconsciously, I reached down and gave my seatbelt an extra tug. Although the show wouldn't air for a couple of days, I had the distinct feeling that life was about to hit warp speed. It was like being on a ride at

Disneyland when I was a child. As the roller coaster climbed higher, and I entered the abyss of anticipation, I'd always double check my seat belt, feel the butterflies of nerves and excitement in my tummy, and think, "Here we go!" That's exactly how I felt as I flew towards home.

CHAPTER 7

One Ringy Dingy

*We ourselves feel that what we are doing is just
a drop in the ocean. But the ocean would be less
because of that missing drop.*

- Mother Teresa

With just a few days to get my ducks in a row until the *Mike and Maty* show aired, it was time to call an all-hands-on-deck meeting with my fledgling volunteers. Two priorities burned brightly. The first was to make sure we had enough people to collect phone calls if the show ended up touching the hearts and minds of the viewers. The voice mail at my home could collect 35 messages at a time. Surely that would be sufficient if we had people pulling messages off at the same time I was speaking with others.

The second was to find a location where we could all watch the show together. Typically, I steer clear of television. Its visuals seem to suck me in magnetically, and I find I'm watching things of absolutely no substance. National Public Radio, newspapers, magazines and the Internet are more than sufficient for info gathering and don't force me to stay glued to the front of a television. We purposely hadn't had television service for years, so watching the show at the ranch house was not possible.

Back in 1996, Parker was a town in flux. Initially, we moved there because it was an equestrian community and land prices were incredibly reasonable, especially compared to the Santa Barbara area we arrived from. As Colorado's population was starting to boom, this horsey hamlet, located twenty miles southeast of Denver, was evolving into a bedroom community.

Josie McHugh was the head of the Parker Chamber of Commerce during this time. Although not the mayor—who was a 27-year-old male with very little interest in a blanket project—she was a powerhouse. Josie was a mover and a shaker and an influential community leader. She was a solid woman, physically and mentally, and when she set her focus on something, it was going to happen.

I became acquainted with her when we were trying to tie all the loose ends for getting Polo in the Park up and running. I'd seen this formidable force in action and watched her break through obstacles like a Sherman tank. When I told her about starting Project Linus, she was immediately behind it one hundred percent. Josie's backing gave the effort the first major, local motivating force to assist with details. Because of her influence in the community, she was able to open doors that otherwise would have taken a lot more effort on my part, especially when it came to publicity and promotion.

As one of Project Linus' early fans, she was able to

coordinate the *Mike and Maty* viewing at a local restaurant, the Warhorse. It was centrally located on Main Street and had a rustic Wild West feel to it. The show aired before lunchtime, so we had the whole restaurant to ourselves. The morning of March 6th arrived, and a dozen of us met at the restaurant. The Project Linus segment was about five minutes in length. The immediate friendship that Eddie and I felt for each other came through—even as far as a thousand miles away. It seemed like a dynamic duo—a young volunteer and a senior news veteran.

I shared the code for my voice mail with my volunteers, and we jubilantly scattered to our respective homes. The drive back to the ranch was ten miles of rural road, and I enjoyed every twist and turn knowing that a great gift awaited me. I just hoped that the show touched the viewers enough that at least some of them would call and be inspired toward action.

Due to the different time zones and airing schedules around the country, the show broadcasted throughout the day. By the time I returned from the Warhorse, the response was already out of control. Ginger had remained at the house and said our phone had been ringing incessantly. When I checked my voice mail, it was already full. With the next ring, I grabbed the nearest notebook and picked up the phone. A female voice on the other end of the line told me she was calling from the Chicago area. She shared a story about when her own child was sick in the hospital and how much she wished that Project Linus had been there for them. She wanted to know an address where she could send a blanket. While she was talking, I heard the click, click, click of call waiting. Others were trying to get through, and although I wanted to hear this caring woman's story, it became immediately apparent that now was not the time to get into conversations.

Plan B was to start pulling messages off voice mail with the skill of a professional administrator. Elissa from Orange County wanted to know where she could send a blanket. So did Christine from Tampa, Vicky from Rockford, Laurie from Harrisonburg, Tammy from Springfield, and Debi from Madison and . . . it went on and on and on.

I copied down names and numbers as quickly as possible. This meant all that day—and for days after—I retrieved voice mails and took copious notes, recording the info the callers left. Many people encountered the full voice mail box and decided to try back later. Bless them! Others gave up, and sadly, we lost them. Unfortunately, it was too early in the game for Project Linus to have a website, so the only way people could get more information about our effort was by phone or by sending a letter to the show. It's estimated that we received over 1,000 calls in the first days following the airing of the show.

A couple hours into the message retrieval regime, Ginger could see I was already getting overwhelmed. He matter-of-factly stated that I needed to come up with a plan other than to have all these viewers send blankets to our ranch. We would soon need a bigger house, unless we could come up with an alternate solution. He was undoubtedly right, and the answer came to me as clear as day.

Fortunately in 1996, there was a fraction of the area codes that exist today, since cell phone usage was just beginning to ramp up. I started highlighting the callers who stated that not only did they love the idea of Project Linus, but they wanted to start this in their own community. I put each potential leader's name down on the top of a piece of paper. Then I copied the names and numbers of all the callers who were from the same area code—and wanted to donate blankets— onto that piece of paper. Soon, I had lists of folks from around the country divided into their own geographical zones—L.A., Seattle, New York City, Houston, Miami, and so on. I then called the person on the top of the list and screened to see if we were "on the same page." This was about making sure the caller was committed to helping us in the long run as opposed to holding a flash-in-the-pan interest.

I wanted to make sure that the potential "coordinators" had the basics: friendly on the phone, sounded like they had a kind heart and were responsible. There was a great deal of trust and gut instinct required, especially as we were first forming. As soon as I felt they were just as eager as I was when I first heard their message, I'd pitch the idea of having them become a chapter coordinator for their area. Some politely declined. They wanted to see it get started locally but didn't want to be the one to do it. There were the demands of time, health, transportation, and money, as well as self-confidence constraints to consider. Many indicated they would be more than happy to make blankets for the person who did decide to step forward.

One caller will always stand out in my mind. A thick, Long Island accent greeted me as I answered Elizabeth Cassidy's call. She mentioned that she would like to see Project Linus formed locally, but when I pitched the idea of having her become the local coordinator, I remember she was a bit leery. Elizabeth stated—with what I soon learned was her witty New Yorker sarcasm—that it was all fine and good for people in the Midwest to do nice things for each other (like make blankets), but it would never fly on Long Island. She was convinced that New Yorkers wouldn't be interested in helping each other in such a way. I felt strongly that she was mistaken in this assumption and knew she'd make a great coordinator.

Rarely, did I feel the need to convince someone that they should be a coordinator. I've learned over the years that if someone isn't excited during the "honeymoon period," they will be much less likely to stick it out when the going gets tougher and more challenging. With Elizabeth, however, I felt strongly that she should head up the effort on Long Island. Gut instinct successfully carried me through much of this period, and Elizabeth's chapter would, in time, become one of the most prolific.

Fortunately, most of the potential coordinators seemed ecstatic to help in any way. That week, some of the nicest people called as a result of the *Mike and Maty* show. Very often, the initial chapter coordinator for an area was the lucky random person who ended up getting through first.

Once they agreed to be a coordinator, I shared the names and numbers of the people in their area. This was a real win-win. The new coordinators didn't have to begin from ground zero and go through a whole song and dance to inspire blanket makers. They started with already-eager Blanketeers who were ecstatic to learn that a chapter had formed in their area and that their blankets would go to local children. Although most were happy to get blankets to any child who would be comforted by their handiwork, it soon became evident that they preferred being able to help within their own communities. One of my favorite slogans, "think globally, act locally" was coming to fruition.

CHAPTER
8

Giant Steps

Obstacles are those frightful things you see
when you take your eyes off your goal.

- Henry Ford

J ust a few days after the *Mike and Maty* airing, boxes started arriving from around the country. The mail carrier, along with UPS and Fed Ex, began making daily stops at our ranch. After a few days of trying to balance bulky boxes, we learned to keep our front gate open, so they could drop off packages at our front porch. It felt like Christmas day after day, as I sat amidst dozens of boxes, waiting to spill forth their mysterious contents. Beautiful blankets of every shape, color and size awaited their release, like a baby chick about to hatch from the confines of its eggy shell. They were knitted, quilted and crocheted and were generously sent by caring volunteer hands.

Occasionally, there were some duds that arrived in the mix. Mostly, they came from smoking households. My nose became quite adept at detecting these culprits, even while still encased in their packages. They spent days in the mail, passed through countless hands, and still reeked of cigarette smoke. I literally cringed as I opened these boxes, knowing that an aesthetically beautiful blanket waited to see the light of day and find its way into the arms of a child. Initially, I would march piles of blankets down to the washing machine to try to extricate the offensive odor.

The last thing a seriously ill child needs is to be presented with a stinky blanket. The washing process worked mildly on the problem. When I learned we were just masking the odor with perfumes that could also be dangerous to a child, especially one with respiratory issues, as well as not effectively removing the harmful chemicals, it became evident that these blankets needed to be immediately weeded out.

Other people sent used blankets, even ones with urine stains on them! My first reaction was, "What were these people thinking!?!" I decided to take the high road, though, and assumed the blanket was given out of the kindness of their hearts. Perhaps this was the only blanket they had, and they were sharing it with us.

As with previous donations, each Blanketeer received a handwritten thank you note. On the ones that had "issues," I tried to educate the Blanketeer of our newly-developing standards: the blanket had to be clean, unused, homemade, free of offending (and dangerous) odors, and without pet hair. As the owner of a veritable menagerie myself, I knew the compelling powers that drew children to blankets seemed to work the same way on animals, especially cats. Many people have cat allergies, and Project Linus did not need to exacerbate any health issues.

Although I felt as if we were getting picky, there were other blanket charities which had far more stringent requirements for their donations. For instance, some would only accept quilts or blankets of a certain size. I wanted people to have fun. If they wanted to try a new pattern, great! If they wanted to use their favorite tried-and-true design— that worked too. Project Linus did not have size, pattern or color requirements. After all, children come in all sizes with all kinds of preferences.

Sometimes, while opening boxes, I was reminded of a story I'd heard years ago. During a college Western Civilization class, my professor explained how Russian commerce worked in comparison to U.S. capitalism. In the United States, if there is a need, there is usually a savvy entrepreneur who is there to fill it. The opposite seemed to be true in Russia, at least at that time.

The story went that, in Russia, some factories were given specifications for what their end product should be. It might be a quantity or it might be to use up the raw materials given to them. The result was either a bazillion tiny pieces that used up very little of the precious resources—but covered the quota for quantity at a minimum of cost—or GREAT BIG parts that would quickly utilize the resources and shorten the manufacturing time. Thus, there were many tiny or a few enormous parts. Rarely, though, was there anything in-between sized. Some of our boxes seemed to apply this same theory. One box might contain dozens of washcloth-sized "blankets," whereas another box would contain one giant king-sized blanket.

With time, a solution to the tiny-blanket problem came from Donna Ridout, our Woodville, Ontario coordinator. She received a call from Orillia Soldiers Memorial Hospital. They requested tiny blankets—16" x 16"—to be used for bereavement. The kits were for newborn babies who had died or were stillborn births. Instead of wrapping them up in a flannel sheet, the facility wished to wrap the babies in a Project Linus blanket made with love and care. This was a more personal touch and helped the parents, family and friends during this most difficult time. At similar facilities, some parents kept the blanket as a treasured keepsake to remind them and others that a tiny family member passed away. Others desired their children be cremated with the blanket as a final show of comfort to the baby.

Another treasure that often appeared in the box was a note. It was particularly intriguing to hear personal stories of why that Blanketeer decided to get involved in Project Linus. Perhaps they had a sick child who might have benefited from receiving a blanket, or they wished someone had made a blanket for them. The most frequent comment was that they were an avid knitter, crocheter or quilter and had run out of family or friends for whom they could make blankets. They were thrilled that their passion could be used to comfort children.

As for recipients, our mission expanded quickly. Children ranging from neonatal to young adult were eligible to receive the blankets. The category of "young adult" afforded us some wiggle-room and the ability to serve individuals beyond a strict age cutoff of 18 years. At one point, there was a cadet at the Air Force Academy in Colorado Springs who had cancer. It was gratifying to be able to assist him with a cozy comforter-cuddle from the civilian world.

March 1996			
Anonymous	Parker, CO	8 quilts	
Becky Crawford	Boulder, CO	15 baby sets	
Marge Durand	Parker, CO	5 quilts	
Heidi Chiacchieri	Parker, CO	1 crocheted	gold & yellow
Helen E Baker	Aurora, CO	9 crocheted	blankets & yard
Mrs. Betty Crane	Aurora, CO	2 crocheted	multicolored
Liz Coats	Aurora, CO	2 crocheted	multicolored
A. Barnhorst	Aurora, CO	1 quilt	yellow w/ clown & balloons
Merrie Valliant	Wheat Ridge, CO	1 quilt	
Charles & Carolyn Rall	Englewood, CO	1 crocheted	wine & spruce
Cynthia Bell	Fountain, CO	2 crocheted	multicolored
Vanderpol	Loveland, CO	2 blankets	
Helen Sinkez	Newark, NJ	1 crocheted & 2 matching pillows	
R. Schwendiman	Holliday, UT	1 tied quilt	Baby Taz
Lynn Doescher	Webster, NY	7 baby blankets	
Jill Cahill	Shelton, CT	1 crocheted	blue & white
J. Ciuppa	Maple Heights, OH	1 crocheted	raspberry & wine
V.E. Wright	Ft. Myers, FL	1 blanket	mint
Pamela Drotts	Topeka, KS	5 crocheted baby blankets	pastels
Sydney Lynne Meade	McDowell, KY	1 quilt	Holly Hobby theme
Anne Komarek	Franklin, NJ	1 crocheted	multicolor
Linda Seidl	No. Lauderdale, FL	1 crocheted	pastel, multicolor

March 1996

Laura Norton	Minooka, IL	1 quilt	From her hope chest!
Sara Hassan	Falls Church, VA	1 blanket	multicolored
Eileen Dankler	Steger, IL	1 crocheted	multicolored granny square
Surayah Hussain	Teaneck, NJ	1 large afghan	rust & white
Susan R. Bird	Buffalo Grove, IL	1 crocheted	black, red, green, white & blue
Maureen A. Weber	Bolingbrook, IL	13 crocheted	made by her & her mother
Cheryl Ogg	Riverton, QY	1 crocheted	red, yellow, green, blue & purple
Shirley Hardin	Castle Rock, CO	1 crocheted	black & multicolored
Bertha Lynn (tv anchor)	KMGH-TV, Denver	1 blanket	pink & blue
Geri Wegrzyn	Alamosa, CO	2 crocheted	
Annie Slocum	Denver, CO	7 baby blankets	
Karen Loucks	Parker, CO	1 crocheted	periwinkle/teal/ white
Mrs. Richard Reed	Benton, LA	1 crocheted	Yummy! Mint, orange, yellow
Theresa Kratschmer	Putnam Valley, NY	1 quilt	Troop #2324 - 2nd graders
Dombrosky & Zitterman	Carbondale, PA	1 quilt	bear & balloons, w/ pink satin trim
Arlene Noles	Wilsonville, OR	1 crocheted	pink/blue & white
Anonymous	Parker, CO	4 crocheted	
Rita Gallagher	Farmingdale, NJ	1 blanket	Ecru w/ peach satin ribbon
Neva Haley	Boulder, CO	1 crocheted	Colorful!

The original goal of Project Linus had been to blanket children with cancer. After the *Mike and Maty* show aired, we received so many blankets and so much interest for children outside the cancer community, that it became necessary to expand the mission. Our goal became, "to provide handmade security blankets to seriously ill and traumatized children."

Boxes and letters continued to roll in. We had more than 20 chapters up and running and making their first deliveries to local hospitals within a couple weeks of the airing. However, it wasn't all smooth sailing.

CHAPTER
9

Growing Pains

*The strongest oak of the forest is not the one that is protected
from the storm and hidden from the sun. It's the one that
stands in the open where it is compelled to struggle for its
existence against the winds and rains and the scorching sun.*

- Napoleon Hill

While studying at the University of Maryland, the journalism students had an inside joke. One dollar, along with our degree, would buy us a cup of coffee, meaning that our major wasn't worth much. I'm sure over the years, that joke has been revised to say "three dollars," now that designer coffee shops like Starbucks have entered the scene. However, with my college major's emphasis on public relations, the information I gained through the university proved priceless for Project Linus.

Almost instantly, I went from a daily routine of morning training with my Masters swim team, random fire department calls, work at the local art framing shop—along with the occasional music tour—to someone with a remarkably clear mission. Like many people, I wanted to find a way to make a positive difference in this world, and find it, I did. With just one television show airing, I now had thousands of people around the country looking to me for direction.

There was never a loss of things to do. I could have been busy 24 hours straight, with all the letters, email and phone calls requiring responses, as well as the boxes of blankets that continued to arrive on a daily basis. The mail carrier began bringing our mail in plastic containers to meet the demand. I was not prepared for the onslaught of activity whipped up by the *Mike and Maty* airing. Prior to the show, I simply hoped to receive some additional blankets that could be shared with other Denver area facilities like Denver Health (then Denver General), Presbyterian St. Luke, St. Joe's, The Children's Hospital, Swedish, St. Anthony's, and the like. Now, I was scrambling to figure out what to do with the thousands of blankets coming in, and more importantly, how to effectively start chapters with coordinators—who were complete strangers—around the country.

My experience as a firefighter/EMT prepared me for the endeavor of running a national charity in many ways. As a scene commander, one is trained to stand back from the situation in order to get a better view of what is going on. If you stay too close to the action, you can miss out on the big picture. I tried to do this on a daily basis by reassessing where we were and what needed to be done next. This is similar to how an airplane pilot continues to tweak the course due to the curvature of the globe and outside forces, such as wind.

In a fire station, everything has a place, and every place has a thing. Hoses go in one area; bunker gear goes in another. Tools have their prescribed location, and trucks are parked in the same spot every time. Although I am not a naturally organized person, by utilizing this method, my life got much easier. I wasn't running around searching for items, and the house was able to maintain relative order. I quickly learned that the computer and phone logs should stay by their respective equipment. Blankets were opened in a prescribed spot with the blanket log, pen and box cutter close at hand. Stationery and stamps needed to stay by the blanket log. Blankets, which had to be labeled, were in one place, close to the sewing box with its blanket tags, needles, thread and scissors.

Blankets already labeled and ready to deliver were counted, bagged and tagged according to size. Recipient locations like St. Joseph's NICU wanted baby blankets, a home for teens wanted larger blankets, and Denver Health and The Children's Hospital required a variety. Items that needed to be sent out to coordinators, like blanket tags, were kept in one place with envelopes and postage. A large white board in my office helped keep count, retained an ever-changing "to do" list, and prioritized the day's events.

Another helpful lesson one learns as a firefighter and EMT is that another person's emergency is not your own. A friend once gave me the book Don't Sweat the Small Stuff... And It's All Small Stuff! How true that is! When focusing on the little things, it's easy to get flustered and discouraged by minute details. I occasionally received a call from an upset coordinator who was in a complete tailspin. By talking things through, she was able to refocus on the mission and move past the speed-bump that seemed like an unscalable mountain just a few moments earlier.

⁓

Fellow Coloradoan, Polly Letofsky, was the first woman to walk around the world. She did this to raise awareness for breast cancer. It had been a dream of hers since she was a twelve-year-old girl. In her book, *3 MPH: The Adventures of One Woman's Walk Around the World*, Polly wrote about her voyage that took her one day short of five years to cross four continents, walk through 29 pairs of shoes and raise millions of dollars for breast cancer awareness. Had she let her concerns about blisters, fundraising or other people's doubts cloud her dream, she never would have been able to accomplish her goal, let alone take that first step. Her motto is "Little steps, big feat!"

There are always the "Debbie Downers" in the world that will try and throw cold water on another person's sizzling dream. Perhaps they do this out of their own fear or jealousy, or they may feel as if they're protecting the dreamer from being hurt. People don't realize how off-putting they can be when a visionary comes to them, entrusting them with their idea. When people say words such as "it will never work," they are not helping, and perhaps their negativism will put a kibosh on something that could truly be remarkable. If, as dreamers, we find ourselves in the midst of a "Negative Nellie," we must plug our ears. They have their own personal agenda, and we should not let it poison us. Who could now imagine a world without airplanes, cars, computers, or even Google? Yet, at one time, these were just a dream too that someone had the guts to bring to fruition.

More than once, I met face to face with a person who tried to squelch the Project Linus dream. They would make comments such as: *"Children don't like homemade blankets. They much prefer store bought ones." "You are going to try to run a national organization from your home?"* "You better watch out, someone may sue you, even though you are trying to do something positive!" I'm so happy I didn't let them stop me in my tracks. Every single invention in this world started with an idea and someone who had the courage to run with it.

The press releases that I sent out to the media were like seeds hitting fertile ground. The media seemed like it couldn't get enough of this grassroots-story-gone-wild. My initial concern of not having enough blankets quickly faded. Finding enough recipient sites became the new focus. Otherwise, we might quickly drown in blankets. The Blanketeers were voracious in their need to produce more blankets. It was like they all had a sweet tooth, and I had just invented sugar. They finally had an unlimited destination for their blanket-making passion and an infinite excuse to shop for blanket supplies, try new color combos, textures and patterns. It was exciting, yet exhausting.

I spent countless hours on the computer answering the same emails over and over and over. *What size blankets did we need? What were our requirements? Where could people send finished blankets? Where did the blankets go? Where could someone make a drop off? What child would receive them?* The questions were never-ending, but what this actually represented, was that word about Project Linus was spreading.

If I could shout back to that scrambling person in 1996, trying to get the Project Linus dinghy—and soon-to-become speed boat—on the right course, I would bellow, "Get a website!" There was no way at the time to know that Project Linus would become the monumental success that it did. For all I knew at the time, this was a one-shot deal. Enthusiasm could just have easily died down after the *Mike and Maty* airing, in the same way a fan section at a football game turns silent after an intercepted play.

In the mid-90's, the Internet was just beginning to boom, so it took longer to understand the full benefits of a website. In hindsight, a lot of time, energy and money would have been saved if an informational site had been up and running a whole lot sooner. Once our website was functioning, anyone who had an interest in our effort could visit and have most of their questions answered immediately. If they wanted additional information, they could then send an email, write a letter, or pick up the phone.

The workload continued unceasingly. While I answered email, others tried to get through the phone lines. Life felt like a constant buzzing from the classic AOL "You've Got Mail" sound of incoming email and the incessant ringing of the phone, which didn't seem to slow down. I was now getting calls from service clubs, moms' groups, scouts, churches and schools, all asking if I could speak to them on Project Linus. My calendar was filling up as fast as the voice mail. Soon after the *Mike and Maty* show aired on television, we expanded our capacity for voice mail to include over one hundred messages and added a second phone line to handle the influx of calls. I was then also able to decipher when a call was personal or business-related.

Because of the media attention and speed of our growth, people assumed we were a funded organization with professional staff available 24-7. Sadly, for the first year, that "assumed" staff consisted mainly of "yours truly." There were several people, like Gretchen LeRoy, who helped whenever possible, but for the most part, it was on my shoulders, and it was starting to wear on me. Not only was much of my time consumed with Project Linus, but many of our personal finances were too. With Ginger being a musician, it meant our funds were often at a feast-or-famine level, depending on when royalty checks came in or new gigs were booked.

This all-volunteer organization was like a baby with a voracious appetite. Barely a day went by without some expense popping up. Ginger never complained about funding Project Linus and even used his "Polo and Jazz in the Park" events to help finance operations once the summer began. After just three and a half months into this fantastic adventure, I began to see the need for some serious organizational changes. It was time to start thinking outside the box and figure out ways to simplify the overwhelming response we were receiving from the community.

CHAPTER 10

Adventures in Success

You may say that I'm a dreamer but I'm not the only one
I hope someday you'll join us and the world will be as one.

- John Lennon

During a blanket-making event, a Blanketeer innocently asked why an all-volunteer effort needed to have a head office and incurred expenses. I assured her that it was vital to have a central location, so everyone could be on the same page, doing things in a consistent way. Although the chapters were encouraged to have their own flair, it was essential that we share some uniformity. We all used the same blanket tags, had the same flyer, and carried out the same mission: getting security blankets to seriously ill or traumatized children. If this had not been so, some chapters might have delivered blankets to nursing homes, others to soldiers, and still others to animal shelters. All are worthy causes, but without a finite mission and a branded look, the effort becomes diluted and is not as effective.

Despite the diversity in the look of a Project Linus blanket, I wanted them all to have a uniform identifier. As a fledgling crocheter, I had come across a company in the back of a craft magazine that made personalized labels. It seemed necessary for all of our blankets to have a singular label to tie them together. Our first labels simply said, "Made with Tender Loving Care by Project Linus." They added another special touch to the work that the Blanketeers were doing for Project Linus and provided a remembrance for the recipients of where their blanket originated. Because of how quickly we were receiving and sending out blankets, I went from ordering them by the dozens, to the hundreds, to the thousands—practically overnight. The cost of the labels was ever-climbing with our increased numbers. They were then repackaged by me and sent to coordinators all over the country.

Even without a paid staff, we couldn't help but incur expenses. The post office does not let organizations mail items for free just because they are doing nice things for people. We didn't seem to qualify for most of the money-saving mailing options. Either we needed nonprofit status (which we hadn't obtained yet), the mail needed to go to one zip code, or there had to be at least 200 identical pieces, or . . . the list went on. These were all requirements Project Linus couldn't reach at the time. Our coordinators and Blanketeers were starting to span the United States and Canada.

In addition to postage, there was the phone bill. Unfortunately, the phone company does not offer free phone usage to such efforts and long distance was much more expensive than it is today. Neither will gas stations fill up our cars for free. Internet services had to be paid for, as well as office supplies, fax machines, and other miscellaneous items. The funding had to come from somewhere and without a sponsor for this nonprofit, that "somewhere" was our personal family fund.

As quickly as Project Linus was becoming a success through its direct efforts and our impact on the children, financially it was draining us. My car seemed to be guzzling gas faster than I could fill it. I drove all over the Denver metro area picking up and delivering blankets, as well as visiting groups to give presentations. Despite being an all-volunteer effort, it was important that we run the organization as professionally as possible.

Considering all the mail delivered to our home, it was a rare occurrence when any of it included a monetary donation. A simple, self-addressed, stamped envelope felt like a HUGE gift! I've always found it difficult to ask for money. Visions of slimy televangelists unabashedly swindling their naive congregants left a sour taste in my mouth for fundraising. I innocently wanted to believe that when we needed money, it would just magically appear.

The Parker post office[1] became an almost-daily destination. Since that time, a zip code has been added, and the building has changed, but much of the staff who watched Project Linus take root, is still there. Stamps and packages for coordinators were the two main reasons for my routine

---

1. If you are ever driving through Parker, Colorado, please stop in at the post office. I guarantee you'll receive top-notch service with a smile—especially if you are served by one of the old timers. (I'm referring to the amount of years they have worked there, not their ages.)

post office visits. I seemed to be forever running out of stamps. I frequently arrived, precariously juggling packages of outgoing blankets, starter kits for new coordinators, and blanket tags for established chapters. This was before the post office had automated doors, and I remember praying that someone would exit as I was going in so they could assist me. Whenever I left the building, however, I felt lighter—not only because I was package-free, but because I knew more children would be blanketed with love in the days ahead. And I had an added skip to my step from that day's encounter with some of the guys on staff.

Contrary to the adage that postal employees are a bunch of nutty government workers, these guys were often the highlight to my day. There were Mike, Rob and John. And then there was Bob. He is a hilarious guy from Connecticut who has somehow missed the talent agents on Jay Leno as a comedian. Everything about Bob is notable; from the way he greets his customers with a hearty and exaggerated, "Hallllllooooo. What can I do you for today?" to the way he wears his pants halfway up to his chest. These men were extremely friendly and supportive of Project Linus.

The constant influx of correspondence was daunting. I often felt as if I was spinning my wheels. The harder I worked, the taller the stack of "things to do" seemed to grow. In fact, the word about Project Linus was spreading like wildfire through the media and Internet. Things often felt as if they were getting out of control. Typically, I can handle anything that is thrown at me. I love getting my hands dirty and figuring things out, and I'm always up for a challenge. The rapid speed, with which Project Linus was growing, however, was even a little daunting for this "I can do it all" woman.

I wish I'd known about Brian Tracy's book Eat That Frog when I was going through this very stressful period. He quotes Mark Twain as saying that if the first thing you do each morning is eat a live frog, you can go through the rest of the day with the satisfaction of knowing that the frog is probably the worst thing that will happen to you all day long.

Tracy explains that your "frog" is your biggest, most critical task—the one you are most likely to procrastinate on if you don't do something about it. It is also the one task that can have the greatest positive impact on your life and on the results you seek. He then explains that the first rule of frog-eating is: "If you have to eat two frogs, eat the ugliest one first." This is another way of saying that if you have two crucial tasks before you, start with the biggest, hardest, and most urgent task first. Discipline yourself to begin immediately, and then persist until the task is complete and before you go on to something else.

Wow—that made so much sense. Yet, I was living in complete contradiction to this advice. Usually, I did the easiest tasks first and then hoped the difficult ones would just disappear in a "poof." Those ugly frogs rarely vanished and sometimes they even grew larger! I used to rely on my predilection for being an adrenaline junkie to get me through in a crunch; thus, my nickname—Last Minute Loucks.

I soon realized that I needed assistance to keep everything on track. Working solo at the ranch was a bit overwhelming, and oddly enough, felt a little claustrophobic. As a people person, I needed to work around others.

Luckily, after speaking with a local women's group, a

member approached me and invited me to check out her women's entrepreneurial group, Netcasters, which had formed at her church. They met weekly to support, encourage, and hold each other accountable as they worked towards their desired goals. Each member was trying to accomplish something different. Robin wanted to be a public speaker. Melissa aspired to be a writer. Gretchen wanted to create religious banners for churches. Barb was a happy homemaker with a focus on her growing family. I was trying to keep my act together with a burgeoning charity. Simultaneously, I felt overwhelmed with all the daily tasks required to keep the effort and me afloat.

Netcasters was my lifesaver. We were able to safely vent our personal hurdles and frustrations and get support from the group. This special group of ladies played a vital role in my sanity and success during the first years of Project Linus. It is one thing to let myself down, but unacceptable to let others down. So, whatever I promised the group, I made sure to do before our next weekly meeting. Soon, I was making more progress and finding my footing again.

CHAPTER

11

Dandelions in the Spring

*Never tell people how to do things. Tell them what to do
and they will surprise you with their ingenuity.*

- George S. Patton

Despite the everyday challenges and growing pains of
starting a nonprofit, truly incredible things began
to happen. We swiftly expanded from supporting
hospitals, to aiding hospice, police & fire departments,
shelters, school counselors, social workers, Ronald McDonald
Houses, Make a Wish Foundation, specialty camps, and
more. The sky was our limit!

My friend Tina, who is also a graphic artist, not only was
my sounding board and huge supporter as I first conceived
of Project Linus; she generously donated her services and
created our initial logo. She also designed our first business
cards with stylized writing. They were colorful, professional

and spunky—just the way I wanted our image to appear. However, they lacked one *"most desired"* ingredient—the Linus image. We still had not received permission to use his likeness—not yet, anyway! This situation wasn't for lack of trying. I routinely contacted United Media, the company who owned the rights to his image. Unfortunately, I didn't seem to be making much headway. The media often inquired about our connection with the blanket-toting Peanuts character, Linus. I would clearly state that we were not in any way connected with the Peanuts gang, although we hoped to have a relationship with them soon. At least, for the time being, the "Linus" of Project Linus was a fictitious child with cancer. The media understood fully—getting a corporate agreement is not the easiest feat to accomplish.

Within a few weeks of the *Mike & Maty* airing, a couple dozen chapters had quickly formed. It was a joy to hear about their successes and community involvement. Before the end of March, the Durham, North Carolina coordinator started deliveries to Duke University Medical Center, the first of the chapters to make an official donation outside of Denver. She also organized a sew-a-thon to collect more blankets. Another early success was when the Chicago chapter was allowed to display blankets throughout the cancer wing of their children's hospital. Patients had the opportunity to peruse the hallway and pick their blankets off the clothesline display. It was wildly popular. When I heard the excitement in the coordinator's voice as she shared the news, I was deeply touched. Her enthusiasm and dedication added fresh kindling to my passion for this project.

The knowledge I gained from my journalism background continued to prove priceless. I was able to share my expertise with chapter coordinators so they could utilize the media to get more donations and raise awareness about Project Linus. I'd done work like this for years, through Ginger's music career and polo events, making it a natural crossover to our nonprofit. A common knee-jerk reaction from new coordinators was fear of the media. They asked questions such as, *"What should I say? How will I look?"* I reassured them that all they had to do was be themselves, talk about Project Linus and share any heartwarming hometown stories they had. People love a painted picture. The media is sometimes challenged to find "good news" stories, and here we were—ready, willing and able to provide beautiful local features wrapped in a cozy security blanket!

It wasn't long before press clippings began to arrive from chapters around the country. Although none of us got into this line of work for the fame or fortune, it was a joy to see these local do-gooders receive public recognition for the service to their community's children. Many of the coordinators spent their lives in the background, quietly doing extraordinary things. This was a time for them to step out from behind the shadows and be seen and heard. For some, this proved to be an uncomfortable position, but they bit the bullet and did it for the team anyway.

Soon, we began sharing in each other's successes around the country:

- The *Houston Chronicle* wrote about husband and wife team, Lash and Kathy McGee, who donated to Texas Children's Hospital, M.D. Anderson Cancer Center, and the Ronald McDonald House. Despite being busy parents with four children ranging in ages from one to nine, they wanted to teach their children to take care of less fortunate people.

- Lisa Gilmer, a Glen Burnie, Maryland coordinator, expressed in a local newspaper interview that she was first inspired by a notice in her church's prayer list about a friend's grandson who had leukemia. That child ended up being the first Maryland recipient of a Project Linus blanket.
- A South Kitsap, Washington team of Amy Fox, and her mother-in-law B.J., shared in their paper that they became involved after watching the *Mike and Maty* show, because it struck a personal chord. When her niece was hospitalized, Amy noticed other youngsters clinging to their blankets as they underwent painful treatments or as they said goodbye to parents who had to go home for the night or get back to work.
- Avid baseball fan, Carol Tornetta, the Reading, Pennsylvania coordinator, let the media tag along as she delivered blankets to Children's Hospital of Philadelphia, accompanied by two members of the Reading Phillies baseball team.
- A picture displaying quilts and 20 smiling students' faces from South Fork Elementary in Likely, California, helped share the news about Project Linus with readers in Sandy Sphar's community.
- North Iowa's coordinator, Deb Wolf, reported to her local *Globe-Gazette* that three of the Wolfs' family friends each had a child with cancer. "Sometimes you feel so helpless; this is something I could do to get involved. This is something anyone can do!"

These personal stories inspired thousands of Blanketeers to flock to our effort. It was like waving a metal detector over a sandy beach and uncovering all kinds of hidden treasures. By May, we donated over 1,000 blankets and had 45 chapters up and running!

In June, I went back to Virginia to celebrate my birthday with my family. I needed a well-deserved break from the phones and computer. While on the East Coast, I made a quick visit to New York City. I had the opportunity to meet with some of my earliest coordinators who lived in the vicinity, including Elizabeth Cassidy of Long Island and other coordinators from Connecticut and Pennsylvania.

Eddie Adams, the writer who inspired Project Linus, met me for brunch. Knowing we would see each other during my stay, I brought him a very special thank you gift—my first, and probably last, crocheted *black* blanket. Although it was quite an eye catcher (since blankets in that color are not the norm) it contained one major challenge. Despite being extremely careful about where I worked on this black beauty, its color—which was Eddie's favorite—made it a magnet for lint. I used a lint roller on it practically until the moment he received it. When I presented him with the gift, he was visibly touched to receive his own tangible piece of Project Linus.

Eddie invited me back to his home to meet his wife, Elyssa, and their son August, the impetus for the *Parade* article. They lived within blocks of what would in just a half decade be known as the infamous Ground Zero. We all spent a beautiful summer afternoon together, taking the Staten Island ferry over to see the Statue of Liberty. Being the consummate photographer, Eddie took some pictures of Ms. Liberty and me. In one of the shots, the Twin Towers are looming in the background. None of us could have fathomed the horror that would occur at that site and how Project Linus would play a role in bringing comfort to thousands in its aftermath. I came back from that trip feeling recharged, refreshed, and renewed with my vision for Project Linus. Once again, I was ready to tackle anything that came my way.

Shortly after I returned from my trip, Ginger and I were selected as the Grand Marshalls for the 25th Annual Parker Days Festival Parade. Ginger was chosen, not only because he was an international music legend, but also because of all he'd done to support local charities and cultural events. I was chosen because Project Linus had already generated a lot of publicity and goodwill for the town. This annual three-day event is a large festival that has managed to retain its hometown feel, with rides, vendors, carnival food and live bands.

During the Saturday morning parade down Main Street, Ginger rode his horses in full polo gear, and I followed in a horse-drawn, Cinderella-style carriage. Feeling a bit uncomfortable in a princess role, I brought two of my favorite sidekicks to ride in the carriage with me, Bertha and Billy, our brother-and-sister dog combo. The crowds loved seeing the dogs in the carriage! The following day, Colorado Senator Ben Nighthorse Campbell, the only Native American to hold such a lofty position at that time, led the 13th Harley Freedom Festival and Street Rod Parade. It was an exciting weekend in our little town of Parker!

All summer long, Project Linus continued to grow like dandelions in the spring. Chapters popped up in big cities and small towns alike. The enthusiasm from existing and new coordinators was absolutely contagious. Although the workload at Headquarters was still heavy, it somehow seemed a little easier due to all the encouraging news. Positive reinforcement is a good motivator.

Letters started pouring in not only from interested Blanketeers and potential coordinators but also from parents whose children had been recipients of our comforters. They were so thankful that someone had taken the time to do something for their child in their time of need. One particular series of letters really touched our hearts. The first contact was a thank you note from a mother of a child with an aggressive cancer. A couple months later, the mom wrote to report that her child was getting progressively worse and her Project Linus blanket was one of the few items that was with her night and day, whether on the couch, in bed or at the hospital. A few months after that, an envelope with a now-familiar return address label arrived. The mom reported that her daughter had since died. They decided to keep her Project Linus blanket on their couch. Anytime a family member felt the need to connect with the young girl, they would wrap themselves in the blanket and feel her spirit. This family's experience was so powerful that it soon became a story I shared during my frequent speaking engagements.

August brought the Olympics, which were held that year in Atlanta, Georgia. Being lifelong athletes, Tina and I were excited to obtain tickets for several events, including track and field, weightlifting and the women's basketball competitions. I flew out to Virginia, and we prepared for an early morning departure and our drive down the coast. As we packed the car that morning, we learned there had been a bombing in the Olympic Square. When friends and family called to ask if we were still going, we both answered with a resounding YES! I couldn't imagine a safer place and time to be attending the Olympics than after a bombing. The area would be crawling with security from all areas of the government.

As we headed down the coast, we met with coordinators in the Raleigh, North Carolina area. It was so gratifying to be able to connect people to the voices I'd been speaking with over the past few months. I'd seen some in newspaper stories but here they were, live and in person! I felt like Patton going out to meet his very successful troops. Every face-to-face encounter made the pulse of Project Linus that much stronger and more vibrantly alive for all of us.

Within weeks of my birth, my mother started shuttling me on a 1,250-mile roundtrip drive between her native Montreal and our home in the Washington, D.C. area. Those early exposures instilled a lifelong adoration of road trips. I love to drive, but when I'm not behind the wheel my hands need to be busy. Tina obliged my request to stop at a Hobby Lobby spotted from the highway, and I picked up some essential items: red, white and blue yarn, an N-sized crochet hook, scissors and a blunt needle for yarn weaving. By the time we arrived in Atlanta, I'd created a blanket that looked like the American flag. Despite the fact that the blanket was missing stars, it didn't take much of an imagination to know we were rooting for Team U.S.A. The blanket became a hit wherever we went. Oddly enough, most of the compliments came from men. Although not planned, our U.S.A. blanket became an effective door opener for conversations about Project Linus.

People simply loved it.

When I returned to Colorado a week later, I washed the blanket and decided to personally deliver it to a special patient. I didn't want to simply drop it off with Volunteer Services as I felt its story would get lost. It felt important to be able to share the story of this particular blanket's Olympics adventure. I felt certain that I would know who was meant to have the blanket as soon as we met. Perhaps it would be a child with pictures of their favorite Olympic athlete plastered on the wall next to their bed. Or maybe they themselves would be an athlete. With absolute conviction, I knew that I would be guided toward that child.

The blanket recipient ended up being an eight-year old boy whose cancer had returned, and he was not at all happy about being in the hospital. As we entered his room, Jake looked skeptically at me and the red delivery wagon with its mountain of blankets. From his body language, I could tell this child was going to be a tough customer. He wasn't interested in picking a blanket, so I decided to do it for him. Drawing upon my EMT experience, I knew the best way to connect with a child is to drop to their eye level rather than appear as a *"menacing giant figure"* towering over them. I pulled up a chair and retrieved the flag blanket from the bottom of the stack where I'd tucked it earlier. I began sharing stories of my Olympic adventure—the thrill of sitting amongst jubilant fans of the Greek weight lifter as he won the gold, witnessing the beehive of activity during the track and field events, and having the hot ticket to one of my favorite Olympic events—women's basketball.

Jake's eyes exuded a flicker of interest which grew as I shared the stories. Within a few minutes, he seemed to visibly lift out of his disheartened mood. When I told him this tri-colored blanket had been at the Olympic Games cheering on a variety of USA teams, he took a keen interest in it and asked if it could be his blanket. After speaking with his grateful parents for a few minutes, I deftly maneuvered the wagon back out to the hall. As I gave a tug on the wagon handle to resume my deliveries, I snuck one last look into his doorway. Jake had spread the red, white and blue colors across his bed and with a smile on his face, was gently petting it like a family dog. The blanket could not cure his cancer, but at least it was bringing him comfort. Jake now had a new story to share that was above and beyond what his latest lab scores were. Success!

By fall, Project Linus had grown to 120 chapters. In a newspaper article, Catherine Tringhese, of Stratford, Connecticut, stated that 800 blankets were delivered by her five-month-old chapter to various locations, including local facilities such as Yale-New Haven Hospital, the Ronald McDonald House and Paul Newman's Hole in the Wall Gang Camp. It was astonishing to think to the obstacle Rocky Mountain Children's Center presented less than a year ago with a goal of 100 blankets. Here were relatively new chapters delivering 800! Project Linus continued to pick up momentum at a very fast pace.

CHAPTER
12

Hearts of Gold, Yarn of Steel

*If you ever need a helping hand, you'll find one at the
end of your arm... As you grow older you will discover
that you have two hands. One for helping yourself;
the other for helping others.*

- Audrey Hepburn

In the early days of Project Linus, I made the mistake
of being overly generous when sharing with new
Blanketeers some of our rarely received, donated yarn.
Occasionally, they seemed to do a disappearing act after
receiving a portion of our coveted stash. Perhaps the project
was intimidating or maybe they just lost interest. I learned
through experience to give a first-timer just enough of this
precious commodity to make one blanket. If they returned
it to me in blanket form, I gladly shared more with them.
Needless to say, I was a little protective of our reserve.

One of the biggest unexpected joys about Project Linus
has been the friendships gained along the way. I received a

call one day from someone who asked if her mother-in-law, Teruko (Teri) Otsuki, could be the recipient of some of our donated yarn. Teri was a crocheter, but as a retiree on a fixed income, yarn was a luxury she couldn't afford. During one of my next delivery runs, I stopped off at Sakura Square, a Japanese-oriented apartment building in downtown Denver where Teri lived. I paid a brief visit to her and dropped off the yarn, with the understanding that she would call me when she completed her blanket. Little did I realize that I had just met a prolific Blanketeer, and someone who would become a dear friend. Literally, the next day, I received the first of many calls from Teri. She finished her first blanket and was ready for more yarn!

On my next visit to town, I brought her enough yarn for a month. We soon developed a routine. I visited Teri at her apartment, exchanged bags of fresh yarn provisions for her completed ripple-crocheted blankets, and then took her to one of the most popular sushi restaurants in Denver for lunch, the Sushi Den. We sat at the sushi bar in front of her grandson who worked there as a sushi chef. For years, she would only allow me to buy her lunch if it was her birthday so I know she really saved her pennies for these lunch dates. Once we finished eating, we headed to local hospitals to deliver blankets. Teri came into the facilities with me and got such joy when she saw how gratefully her blankets were received. To top it off, the Volunteer Service staff and nurses were always gracious and helped make Teri feel like the hero she was. Occasionally she got to meet the patients and their appreciative parents, leaving a long-lived smile on her face.

Over the years, Teri's mobility diminished. It became difficult for her to enter the hospitals, so she chose to stay in the car while I dashed in for a delivery. Teri still enjoyed going for lunch as well as the opportunity to be out in the world and people watch. If I could wave my magic wand, I would start another charity and take mobility-impaired and transportation-challenged people out for rides. Knowing how much these excursions meant to Teri, I believe others would appreciate and benefit from such a service. How fun it would be to have a sidecar on my motorcycle and take them for rides through picturesque canyons or by a beach. One can always dream!

One day, while my parents were out for a visit, we noticed Teri was not her typical self. She seemed a bit distracted. As my father and I assisted her on the sidewalk, she made a slow and steady melt to the ground. Her dutiful granddaughter Tracie was with us and guaranteed that she would follow up on Teri's medical condition. Shortly after that incident, family and friends began to occasionally find her on the floor in her home. It was the classic, "Help! I've fallen and I can't get up" story. It seems that Teri's doctor had put the fear of breaking a hip into Teri, so she decided to super-dose her vitamin D, which produced stroke-type symptoms. It became apparent that Teri could no longer live alone.

Teri continued making blankets, even after she moved to a nursing home. Despite the limited space in her shared room, there was always a place for her blankets. She confided in me that before Project Linus came into her life, she genuinely felt she was simply taking up space in the world. Although she had a terrific family, she didn't feel she was contributing. Until Project Linus, she just ate, watched television and waited for family visits.

With Project Linus, her routine was much the same;

however, now it was infused with an activity that made a positive difference in the life of a child. Each day, she woke, crocheted, ate breakfast, crocheted, watched television, ate lunch, crocheted, watched television, ate dinner, then crocheted and watched television until it was time to go to bed—usually around 7:30 p.m. Teri was quoted in the *Rocky Mountain News* in January of 1997 as saying, "I enjoy crocheting, especially for these children. I plan on doing this until I can crochet no more—and I hope that's a long time."

She developed a sizeable fan base for her work and efforts with Project Linus. It was impossible not to love her kind and gentle spirit. One day, *9 News* called to let Teri know she had won a Hero Award for her work with Project Linus and asked when they could come over to videotape her for a news piece. In classic modest response, Teri politely declined, stating that awards were not why she made her blankets. It was all about the children. Over the years, she kept an active tally that reached well into the hundreds.

Teri was genuinely interested in everyone's lives and had an uncanny ability to remember names and dates. At her funeral, I learned that many others received an early-morning "Happy Birthday" call from Teri every year on their special day. As many seniors do, Teri lived a different schedule than the rest of us—early to bed and early to rise certainly applied to her. When our phone rang at 6 a.m., it was usually a call from Teri, needing more yarn and, when appropriate, a birthday greeting. What a way to start the day! Even after her passing, when we received an early morning hang-up call, we lovingly joked that Teri must be out of yarn again!

Each chapter has its own unique troop of Blanketeers. These volunteers donate anywhere from a single blanket to thousands during their time with Project Linus. Sometimes, it's the Blanketeers' personalities that make them stand out from all the other volunteers. Other times, it may be the sheer volumes they produce. Dorothy Dravet, a coordinator from Northwest Indiana, had two extraordinarily distinctive Blanketeers who kept her on a constant quest for more yarn. This dynamic duo made anywhere from 26-30 blankets each month! Even for an avid crocheter, that's a lot of blankets, and a whole lot of yarn.

Alice Dice is another of the Denver superstar Blanketeers who continues to be fully involved. She started volunteering while working at Lockheed Martin. She got her co-workers to donate Beanie Babies and other small stuffed animals. These were an added touch that she included with her blanket donations. Her entire basement was transformed into a Project Linus craft area. There are closets with special shelving to hold fabrics and batting. Some of it is donated, other she donates herself. Alice has held many quilting bees in her basement. She and her quilting partner Catherine Westlake have been responsible for thousands of blankets. Whenever there is a crisis, they are ready, willing and able to take on a special task. Alice's husband is a great sport when it comes to the flurry of activity that regularly occurs in their basement.

Another extraordinary Blanketeer entered my life after an article about Project Linus ran in the *Denver Post*. I received a call from a woman who wanted to donate some blankets. As was the case during that time, I ventured out to make the pickup. Every bell and whistle went off in my head as I made my way down the dimly lit staircase to the basement level, then down to the end of the hallway to the apartment. The smells of a variety of cultures' culinary endeavors, along with the infused odors of rotting trash and urine, permeated the air.

When the door opened, it was as if the doorway was back-lit by a heavenly light. The occupants, a middle-aged couple, lived in the tiny one-bedroom space. They proudly shared with me that everything in their apartment had been obtained through dumpster diving. Even their bed, which was a large scrap wood board balanced atop cinder blocks, and their "mattress" reminded me of a Dagwood sandwich— many layers of a multitude of blankets. When I gave Mary some of our donated yarn, she quickly spun it into a beautiful blanket. She and her husband struggled with their own life and health obstacles, yet their hearts were full of gold. They felt that it was their honor to assist the children through the donation of handmade blankets.

I confessed to Mary that I was uncomfortable delivering blankets to one particular facility. Denver General was the hospital that catered to the indigent population of the city and, in fact, served the child population that most needed Project Linus blankets. According to a recent newsletter received from this facility, every year nearly 4,000 babies are born at this hospital—90% of them into families who live below federal poverty levels. These families have few resources and little or no discretionary income. As a result, many of them are forced to choose between items of necessity for their babies, such as diapers and car seats; and other pressing responsibilities, such as rent and groceries. Some of the patients at Denver General literally had nothing. A number of the babies left the hospital wrapped in only a smuggled hospital blanket or towel, because the parents had no clothes for their little ones.

The Denver General parking lot felt as if I stepped into a third-world country—women squatted in the throes of giving birth, prisoners in leg irons being escorted by prison guards, and gang members. It was a scary place back in the 90's, to say the least. Parking was far from the front doors and deliveries were a logistical nightmare. Dragging overstuffed and heavy bags of blankets through the parking lot and the halls to the Volunteer Services Center was physically and mentally challenging.

When I confided my discomfort with delivering to Denver General, Mary quickly volunteered to make the delivery herself. Not having a car, she merrily hopped on a bus from her own questionably safe neighborhood and rode to the other side of town to make the donation. She was truly a blessing to our effort and to the children who received those blankets. In time, our deliveries were far more than just a few bags, and too much for one person to handle alone on a bus. Mary eventually fell off the radar, but during her time with us, she proved to be a superhero.

I had a conversation with Eddie Adams once about his experience as a photographer in the heart of war zones. He witnessed bullets whizzing past him and people killed next to him. I asked him, "Weren't you ever afraid for your life?" He shared with me that he felt as if his camera was his shield and it always protected him from harm.

I started to employ this same philosophy when delivering to Denver Health. No longer were the bulky bags of blankets a vulnerability; they became my shield. With this new outlook, I started to meet some interesting people. Folks tattooed and pierced from head to toe—as well as others my sixth sense wanted to avoid—would go out of their way to help me bring the bulky bags into the hospital. It was pretty ironic that although I was there to help ease the weight of their children's sorrows, they offered to help lighten my load. Denver General, which is now called Denver Health, has become one of my favorite recipient sites.

It was incredible to see how the Project Linus ripple effect infused the lives of the Blanketeers and coordinators alike. Elizabeth Cassidy, our Long Island coordinator, was a prime example of this. I didn't realize when I first spoke with her, that Elizabeth had hurdles of her own to overcome. She used to work in the highly "looks-oriented" fashion industry in New York City. After a mildly disfiguring auto accident, Elizabeth lost confidence in her ability to speak in front of people. She quit her job in the city and settled into the safe suburbs. Speaking about Project Linus in front of senior citizens was something she was able to pull off with relative ease. She knew they were beyond scrutinizing a "flawed" exterior. While she was at the helm as coordinator of the Long Island area, her chapter was one of the most prolific. Through her work with Project Linus, Elizabeth was able to pull herself out of a life blip, make changes, and even become a life coach.

It became blatantly obvious that Project Linus was on a huge growth path and was not going to peter out after the *Mike and Maty* show aired. That show served as a mere jumpstart that got the effort kicked into high gear. Our next major win was the development of our website. Craig, the husband of our Lincoln, Nebraska coordinator, Bobbie Connolly, offered his web-building skills to our effort.

Back in the mid-1990's, it seemed that those with websites were mainly corporations and celebrities. It was as if a degree in computer programming was required to tap into the scary frontier of the cyber world. Nowadays, almost anyone with a basic knowledge of computers can have their own Facebook page up and running within minutes. Having our own website not only added to our credibility, but it proved to be a remarkable tool. As soon as it was live, a large percentage of the daily correspondence dropped off. People hadn't lost interest in us—they were finally able to obtain our information through a very effective medium. The senior population was one of the last to join the computer world, so their letters and calls continued to find their way to the ranch, but it was at a much more manageable pace. People were able to get the information they needed anytime or from anyplace, even at 3 o'clock in the morning.

What incredible achievements we were able to attain that first year!

CHAPTER
13

Saving the Starfish

To accept good advice is but to increase one's own ability.

- Johann Wolfgang von Goethe

P roject Linus was growing by leaps and bounds, and
for the most part, the entire Headquarters' work was
still being done by me. Despite our rapid growth and
my continued commitment to this organization, I sometimes
questioned my dream to provide blankets to so many children
in need. It seemed that the world was full of a never-ending
need for our product. What I would have loved more than
anything else was for all the world's problems to go away—
no more hunger, no more disease, no more abuse, no more
war. Without the miracle of all miracles happening, however,
Project Linus was going to be in business for a long time to
come.

The world was filled with children in need of comfort. Our mission was so vast and coped with such devastating stories—children with disease, those who had lost a parent due to military service, and those who came from abusive homes. Sometimes, it was very disheartening to hear the stories. Were we really making a difference? But then one remembers the story of the starfish.

Every day, an old man walked the beach with a pail, picked up starfish that had been washed in by the tide and threw them back into the sea. One day, a young boy stopped the old man and asked, "Why do you throw the starfish back? It doesn't matter. They will only wash up on the shore again tomorrow." The old man picked a starfish out of his pail, threw it as far as he could into the sea, and replied, "It mattered to that one.

If we were "mattering" to just one child, then all the hard work and frustration was worth it.

My personal theme song is, "Walking on Sunshine," and it is the way I choose to live my life. I have a strong belief that our attitude has a lot to do with how we get through life. One of my favorite recent emails came from my friend Margaret Hanssler who, with her mother-in-law Mary, is a frequent Project Linus helper. The email eloquently conveyed a message about attitude:

"A woman woke up one morning and looked in the mirror. There, she spotted three hairs on her head. 'Great!' she exclaimed. 'I think I'll braid my hair

today!' And she had an excellent day.

"The following morning she woke up and had two hairs on her head. 'Excellent!' she said. 'I think I'll part my hair today!' And she had a fabulous day.

"The next morning she awoke to one hair on her head. 'Yippee!' she chirped. 'I think I'll wear a ponytail today!' And she had an outstanding day.

"The next morning she awoke to not a single hair on her head. 'Wahoo!' she stated with glee. 'I don't have to do my hair today!' And she proceeded to have her best day ever."

People often gave me advice. Some of it I took; other advice I let dissipate like morning fog. One helpful warning came early in Project Linus' days. I met with the Chamber President Josie over lunch one day at Chez Monet, a classic French restaurant in Parker. I distinctly recall her leaning across the table and prophetically warning me about others who would come along when Project Linus became a success.

"Karen, I need to warn you about something," she told me. "It's important that you realize there are two types of people you need to look out for on this journey." She'd experienced this herself with the Parker Days festival. She built up the event to something quite distinctive and felt that others were trying to steal it back from her, now that it was a success. "The first type," she explained, "tries to destroy a successful organization; the second tries to steal it." Both types she told me about that day certainly did appear. Fortunately, the former left as quickly as she arrived (and is no doubt wreaking her havoc on another organization). The latter continues to be a thorn in the Project Linus paw to this day. One of my ongoing wishes is that people use their "forces" for good in order to make our world a better place. Life is simply too short to use our energies otherwise.

A few weeks later, a second predictive person, Diana, called. She requested that I pick up some blankets the members of her Quaker church (also called the Religious Society of Friends) had made for Project Linus. At the time, I'd begun setting up drop-off sites so I wouldn't have to spend as much time picking up blankets. I strategically chose sites around the Denver metro area to make it convenient for the Blanketeer as well as for me to be able to swing by as I was out and about. Sometimes they are taken to homes and other times to public places like Front Range Bank, the yarn store called the Strawberry Tree or Artfully Yours- the framing shop in Parker where I worked. My friend Susan Bell qualified for both categories by welcoming blankets at her home near Denver's popular Wash Park and at her art gallery Bell Studio Gallery.

I felt a strong urging however that I should make an exception for this pick up. I've always been fascinated by world religions and wasn't aware that I had ever met a Quaker. While studying theology, I had learned that my personal beliefs were most closely aligned with those of the Quakers yet I had never pursued that avenue. I giggled with a glimmer of hope that she might be dressed in garb similar to that of the figure on the infamous box of oats. Diana also lived fairly close to me so I concluded it would be a rather easy and interesting pickup.

When I arrived, not only did she a stack of exquisite quilts, Diana also had some excellent advice for me. After the initial pleasantries, she asked me to sit with her in her parlor. She gingerly plunked her large frame, that was clad in modern clothing, into an easy chair, and a total peace seemed to enter the room. In a calm voice, she quietly laid the future of Project Linus out in front of me.

"Project Linus is going to be a huge success. You will be responsible for thousands, possibly millions of blankets. This effort will have a positive ripple effect, touching many lives. You are a people person and a visionary," she said with relaxed surety in her voice. "*You need* to stop burying your skills in the daily chores of email, mail, and phone calls. *You need* to be out in front of people. *You need* to work with the press, meet with groups that could potentially make blankets or support the making of blankets. *You need* to communicate with schools, scout troops, churches, and civic groups."

"Karen," she finished, "if you want Project Linus to achieve its maximum potential, you can't be bogged down by office administration."

I realized immediately that her arrows of advice had hit the bullseye. As an extrovert, I was in my element when surrounded by people. I felt truly comfortable with public speaking and enjoyed watching the audience catch the Project Linus "fever." Motivating the community to action was an enormous thrill. That was the energy behind what started Project Linus in the first place—my love for people, especially children, and a desire to make a difference. I knew I wasn't tapping into my true skills.

It was the first real indication that I should also be hand-delivering these blankets any time I could. I'd previously witnessed that many people were delighted to make blankets for the kids, but it broke their hearts to meet the actual recipients. It was always a surprise to me when I witnessed a Blanketeer break down in the hospital hallway after meeting one of the pediatric patients, since it brought me such pleasure to have time with these children and see their faces light up at the gift. For me, it felt tremendously empowering to make a difference in their lives. Project Linus was a team effort; however, and if others found it difficult to deliver the blankets, that was OK. I was honored to pass along the handiwork of the tender-hearted Blanketeers.

I was thrilled that I had made the decision to pick up the blankets personally that day. During our brief visit, this complete stranger was able to clearly spell out things that instinctually I already knew but hadn't purposely focused on yet. Project Linus was desperately in need of someone who could take care of the behind-the-scenes work. Although several people had helped along the way, no one person had stepped forward on a consistent basis to serve that specific role. In order for Project Linus to grow most efficiently, I needed to focus on my true talents and find someone who was gifted in the areas that I lacked. I jumped at the next opportunity to find that remarkable person.

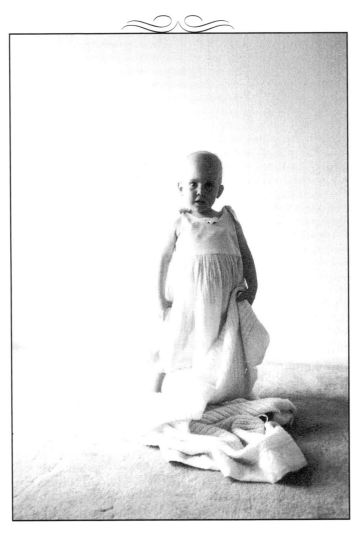

Laura Williams - the image that became the inspiration for Project Linus

(Above) The first Project Linus Headquarters (Left) Meeting with Dr. Arrenson at Rocky Mountain Children's Center with Marge Durand (Below) Note from Vanna White

2-5-96

Dear Karen,

Here is a baby blanket I crocheted for your project. I wish you all great success!

♡

Vanna White

VANNA WHITE

(Above) Ken Mason and Brenda Landau with baby Grant, the night before the Mike and Maty airing (Right) With Mike and Maty in Los Angeles (Below) Warhorse Inn Restaurant, site of Mike and Maty viewing, with gift of donated quilt

(Above) First chance
to meet a group of
coordinators while in
New York City
(Left) With Eddie in
New York (Below)
North Carolina
Coordinators on the
roadtrip to the Olympics

(Above) Karen and Tina Taylor at Eddie Adams' Barnstorm event (Right) Teruko "Teri" Otsuki with her grandson (Below) Sewing Labels

(Above) Acres Green Elementary School made theme blankets that teamed with books they were reading and signed for the blanket recipient (Left) Karen's parents, Valerie and Charlie, at a Quiltmaker Magazine quilting day (Below) HQ's staff left-right, LDS Public Relations Margi Evans, Secretary Shirley Hardin, Quilters Kathryn Reeves and Nan Mell, V. P. Betsy Elliott Front Row, Special Asst Laurie Hoffman, Treasurer Cindy Guthrie, Karen

Erin went from recipient (Above) to Blanketeer in less than a year (Right) (Below) 13-year-old Jerod with his blanket

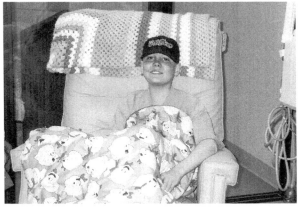

117

(Above) Meatloaf signing a
quilt square for a fundraiser
(Above Left) Meatloaf's
signed quilt square (Left)
In Aspen with Tennis Star
Andrea Jaegger who has a
camp facility for kids with
cancer called The Silver Lining
Foundation (Below) Ringo
Starr with Ginger (Ringo and
his wife Barbara Bach donated
a blanket)

(Above) Katrina in her photo shoot for Parade *magazine (Right) Friend Melanie's boys with Kory and Kai on the* Parade *photo shoot day (Below) First Project Linus conference*

(Above) Young volunteer siblings Grant, Lauren & Austin(Left) Making blankets (Below) Blanket Day event for the LDS Church

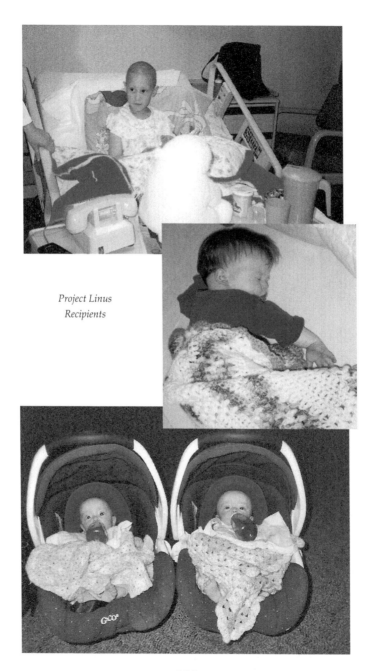

*Project Linus
Recipients*

121

*(Left) Karen posing with
her favorite ride with quilt
made by Frank Lawson
(Below) Karen's husband
Gary working on an Appirio
volunteer day project*

(Above) Young blanketeer gives a test hug (Right) Make A Difference Day event, Fall 2010 with Wendy Evangelista, and junior Blanketeers (Below) "I think I found the Great Pumpkin!"

(Above Left) Northern Virginia's JoAnn "Grammi" Holley (Above) Mobile's Pam Pulley (Left) College roommate Jill Canipe Malcolm who became a Maryland coordinator and went to Oprah with Karen (Below Left) At national conference with mother-daughter dynamic duo Avis Griffin and her daughter Sally Burns (Below) Idaho Coordinator Donna Aten

(Above) Ft. Worth Coordinator Judy and husband Jess "Sweet Thang" Bell (Above Rright) Dayton's Mary Sue and Roy Davis (Right) Kansas City Coordinator Patty Gregory and husband John (Below) North Carolina Coordinator Sandy and husband Lew (Below Right) Karen with Lincoln, NE Coordinator Bobbie and husband Craig "Web King" Connelly

(Above) Getting picked up for the Oprah show with (Left to Right) Joni and Betsy (Left) Letter from Oprah

"Only the emptyhearted lament those days of carnival and renown once they're gone. A man's gift maketh room for him, and bringeth him before great men. This, I believe, is the elation for which he is born."

— Monte Charles Schulz

(Above) Karen was a guest at Charles Schulz' Celebration of Life services in Santa Rosa, CA (Right) Letter from Charles Schulz' grandchildren

CHARLES M. SCHULZ - CREATIVE ASSOCIATES
ONE SNOOPY PLACE
SANTA ROSA, CALIFORNIA 95403

February 15, 2000

Dear Project Linus Friends:

Thank you so much for the warm and cozy security blankets you made for us. It was very kind of you.

Best wishes to you always.

Sincerely,

Grandchildren of Charles M. Schulz

Current Project Linus leadership (Above) Project Linus President Carol and husband, Kirk Babbitt - Director of Development (Left)Vice President Mary and husband, Terry Balagna - Secretary (Below Left) Jane Lawrence - National Treasurer (Below) Betsy - National Assistant extraordinaire and husband, Mark Elliott (Not pictured Chad Lowe - Webmaster)

(Above and Right) Neice of Project Linus blanketeer at the Parker Days festival (Below) The evolution of Project Linus blanket tags

Sending Out an SOS

If you can dream it, you can do it.

- Walt Disney

R unning any small business can be emotionally taxing, to say the least. It is vital to put a support system in place. That support system finally arrived shortly into the new year of 1997. When Denver's *Rocky Mountain News* called for an interview, I quickly put a game plan together. Instead of simply focusing on blankets and the children we were serving, a very definite agenda was formulated—get help! As the reporter quizzed me with the classic journalistic questions of who, what, where, when, why and how, I repeatedly peppered my answers with the need for additional helping hands to assist with the administrative duties that were making me feel like an abandoned sailor in a sea of crushing waves.

While photographer Steve Nickerson was snapping pictures of me wrapped in a landslide of beautiful blankets, a sympathetic image emerged in print. I was so glad the picture was in black and white; otherwise, the readers might have easily spotted how utterly exhausted I was. The stress was starting to take its toll on my well-being. Typically being a strong and healthy person, I found myself fighting back-to-back colds. My glassy eyes may have conveyed sincerity and perhaps wistfulness to the readers, but I could see the telltale signs of fatigue. Writer Shelley Gonzales did a superb job and composed a heartwarming story that inspired many to action, yet it didn't directly mention the need for an assistant. Or so I thought.

Although the words weren't specifically spelled out, the message rang clear to one reader. Shortly after the article appeared, I received a call from a soft-spoken person in Highlands Ranch, a neighboring community to Parker. She said that she would love to help with whatever needed to be done. Her only stipulation was that she wanted to stay behind the scenes. She didn't want to get in front of cameras. Betsy Elliott had made her arrival! She visited me shortly after the call and scooped up an armload of paperwork. Thank you notes to write—*no problem*! Email and letters to answer—*on it*! Betsy was truly the answer to my prayers.

As the chapters grew across the country and more Blanketeers started volunteering their time and resources, I looked for creative ways to work around our under-funding. My initial thought was to get a discount for our volunteers from the stores where they bought materials for the blankets. I approached the manager of the neighborhood Hobby Lobby, a large craft store, to ask if we could get some type of regular discount. He asked if we had a 501(c)(3) status. I'd never heard of such a thing. I soon discovered that it was an IRS designation for a specific type of nonprofit. It became clear that Project Linus needed to get one if we wanted to be considered as a professional effort.

Luckily, one of Ginger's polo buddies was married to an attorney, Jerry Burke. She was a kind woman and exceedingly accommodating when I asked if she could help us get our nonprofit status. Although we had to pay hundreds of dollars in filing fees, she was amazingly generous and donated the work to us "pro bono"—meaning free! We were so grateful, since every donation of any kind was what kept Project Linus going. It took a number of months to receive the status. During that time, we were able to work under the umbrella of an existing nonprofit, The Phoenix Foundation. They were a foundation which worked to help animals but expanded their mission statement to include children.

When the nonprofit status came through, we received a 10% discount at the craft store. Although it wasn't a huge savings, every bit helped and we were grateful for whatever break we could get on materials. Obtaining a nonprofit status helped in a number of ways. First was our ability to save money by not paying taxes when we bought blanket-related items at the store. Our nonprofit status gave people an additional reason to donate to our cause, since their donation could now be tax deductible. It also provided the "credibility factor." People knew we'd jumped through governmental hoops to obtain this status and could trust that we were probably on the up and up. We guard our nonprofit status like treasures in Tut's tomb. The last thing we want is to lose it.

Two of the stipulations for nonprofit status required that Project Linus have a Board of Directors and an annual Board meeting. This ended up being a colossal saving grace. No longer did it feel like I was treading water by myself in the middle of the ocean. I now had official Headquarters teammates! Since my group of friends was quite talented, the Board was formed with me as President, Betsy as Vice President, and Shirley (my swimming/hooker friend) as Secretary. Another swimmer friend, Cindy Guthrie—who happened to be a bookkeeper—became our Treasurer, and Laurie Hoffman came on board as a Special Assistant. Shaun Gann served as our Public Relations specialist. Ginger was made Board Member at Large. With our nonprofit status, our Board, and the addition of an efficient website created and maintained by Craig, we started to roll along like a professional organization.

With Project Linus' growth, many coordinators asked about using the Linus image for brochures, letterhead, and business cards. Despite receiving a letter in February from Charles Schulz stating, "I am willing to do anything that meets with the approval of United Media and wish you continued success with the project," we still didn't have approval to link the image of Linus to our efforts. For the time being, we continued to say Linus was a fictitious child with cancer who'd received a blanket from us—*wink-wink*.

It's understandable that United Media had reservations

about giving us rights to the image. After all, proprietary imagery is one of the ways they earn their money. I can only imagine how often they are asked to give permission for the use of their ever-so-popular characters—Charlie Brown, Snoopy, Lucy, Pigpen, Peppermint Patty, Schroeder, Sally, The Red Baron and, of course, Linus. Fortunately, we were too busy to spend much time lamenting over the waiting game. We had work to do, and this work would eventually prove to United Media that we were worthy of being bestowed with user rights for Linus. By July, United Media would finally agree to let Project Linus use their loveable little cartoon character. Legalities would need to be worked out, but we were getting incredibly close to having Linus on our blanket tags.

Although coordinators were receiving a lot of local publicity, nothing had happened nationally for about a year and a half, not since the *Mike and Maty* show. However, as the old saying goes, "when it rains it pours." *Family Circle* published a flattering article in July that seemed to bring a lot of new interest to the cause. Elizabeth Cassidy told me that when she saw my picture, she laughed with her boyfriend Walter. "Wow," she said, "that's the first time I've seen Karen with lipstick!" My alma mater magazine from The University of Maryland's College Park printed an excellent write-up about Project Linus. This article had a particularly significant meaning, since my father and I are both Terrapin alumni. I heard from classmates I hadn't been in touch with for years, some of whom were actively involved in the media. They were able to use their clout to pull strings for us. What began to happen was a welcome dousing of national attention!

Next, we received invitations to two television shows in

one week. I flew to New York to be on the *Fox After Breakfast* show with Vicki Lawrence of the *Carol Burnett Show*. Having grown up watching that show, I was a huge fan of Carol and Vicki's brilliant comedic talents. It was a lot of fun to share the spotlight with Long Island coordinator Elizabeth Cassidy whose witty banter made the show even more entertaining.

Other guests on the show that day included actress Jeneane Garofalo and actor Christopher Lawford, (Peter Lawford's son, and Cheryl Tieg's husband). Less than a week later, I flew out to Minneapolis to be on the *Everyday Living* show. Although that was a cable show and only aired in limited cities, it still helped build our name and boost my confidence with the television media. With each invitation, we obtained more credibility for Project Linus. Our resume was growing, and new Blanketeers were lining up in droves!

After returning from the second show, I took a road trip to South Dakota with a couple of girlfriends. We attended several days of a Sundance ceremony on Rosebud Reservation, where I was able to present blankets to the children who lived there. Additionally, we delivered blankets to a social worker at Pine Ridge Reservation, a much larger neighboring reservation. Many of the reservation residents lived in substandard conditions. Although the children appeared to be well taken care of, they unquestionably lived in poverty. Medical care was a challenge on the reservation, along with high rates of unemployment and alcoholism. The deplorable housing and road conditions on the reservation were just as discouraging. It was incredible that our country's native people were still living in such squalor.

As children in Northern Virginia, we frequently went on field trips to Washington, D.C. Visiting the White House, going to the National Zoo and the Smithsonian buildings were outings I assumed every American child experienced. One of my favorite scenes in the Museum of Natural History, besides the African bull elephant which has stood for decades in the rotunda of the museum, was that of the Native Americans. I would stand in front of the protective glass case and daydream that I was one of the natives sitting outside my teepee. It was with much sadness when I learned that my family lineage didn't include a single drop of Native blood. Yes, we had Pilgrim blood. No, we did not have any Native blood. The closest we got to a Native lineage were relatives Joan and John Carrington of Wethersfield, Connecticut, who were executed by hanging in 1651. Although they reportedly confessed to "entering a pact with the devil," the probable reason they were hanged was due to their friendship and the commerce they shared with local tribes. The indigenous peoples were considered heathens and therefore devilish.

It was with much regret when my travel companions insisted we depart and attend the nearby annual Harley event at Sturgis. Even though I have had a lifelong love of motorcycles, I hated to leave the spiritual ceremony that was unfolding at Rosebud. I look forward to the privilege of being invited to another Sundance someday. In the meantime, Project Linus' Denver Chapter continues to assist the indigenous children through such groups as the Southwest Indian Foundation in Gallup, New Mexico, which serves the Hopi, Zuni and Navaho tribes. Whenever we have volunteers who plan to travel through South Dakota, we load their vehicles with blankets for Rosebud and Pine Ridge.

When I returned to Parker, the classic onslaught of mail awaited my arrival, plus additional pieces resulting from the two television airings. Most were from interested Blanketeers. One unassuming envelope in particular caught my attention once opened. It contained a handwritten note on a piece of lined, yellow legal paper. It was from the actress and activist Jeaneane Garofalo. She and I had struck up a conversation in the hair and makeup room at the *Fox After Breakfast* show. I had no idea who she was except that she shared a similar passion for dogs. She wrote a kind note of encouragement about Project Linus. She stated that her mother was also a knitter in Pennsylvania and enclosed a monetary gift. It was a considerate and unexpected gesture.

Soon, other funding started to trickle in, including help from mega-biggies like Kmart and Walmart. Occasionally, they cut us a check for a few hundred dollars, but usually they gave store credit. This was helpful too, as it allowed us to stock up on much-needed office supplies and blanket-making materials.

On August 3, 1997, an event occurred that shook the world—Diana, Princess of Wales' death. Not only did her demise come with speculation of foul play by royalty, but also an ardent debate about paparazzi. It seemed the world was in mourning during that time. Perhaps not so much that a princess had been lost but more that we had one less humanitarian hero to slay the dragons of poverty and illness. Diana was someone who understood the power of her celebrity status and used it to make a positive difference in the world. She assisted with such efforts for the treatment and research for cancer, helping the homeless, those with leprosy, AIDs and anything child related. I soon realized that people work their way through grief in a number of ways. Patricia Inman, our Lawrenceville, New Jersey coordinator, received a unique blanket. It was a large crocheted afghan, with a castle knit into the design in memory of Princess Diana.

It was also through grief that some coordinators found their way to Project Linus. Patty Gregory, our Kansas City coordinator, had lost a niece to brain cancer. One day, while watching Alex Anderson on an HGTV quilting show, she saw a segment on Project Linus. She knew immediately that she needed to get involved. "We are all compassionate people," Patty shared, "and when we see a need, we feel we have to do something." Project Linus became such a driving force for Patty that her Christmas letter included, "I have found my purpose."

Communication with some of our coordinators was becoming a challenge. Home computers weren't nearly as prevalent as they are today, and at least a third of the coordinators did not have an email address. We spent many hours calling people with time-sensitive news, such as an upcoming appearance on a television show. Usually, there wasn't a lot of lead time on those events—sometimes we were called with only one day's advance notice. The act of phoning all the email-less coordinators was an enormous time-gobbling job.

We established a Regional Director system to help disseminate fast-breaking information. This required that we select experienced and reliable coordinators in certain regions and make them responsible for passing on news to as many as 20 chapters in their area. Implementing this strategy meant that the Regional Coordinator had significantly fewer calls to make than the person at national headquarters, who would have been obligated to reach over a hundred individuals. As time went on, everyone was required to have an active email address and access it regularly. It seems obvious now, but in the 90's, the Internet was just revving up.

CHAPTER
15

Healing Hands

*The best and most beautiful things in the world cannot be
seen or even touched— they must be felt with the heart.*

- Helen Keller

Were you to speak with a Project Linus coordinator, chances are they would share an "angel story" with you. Some of these stories took place around the holidays when—after emptying their coffers for the year—a heart-wrenching narrative ensued. Perhaps it is a family whose home was just burned to the ground and the children lost everything, including their favorite teddy or blanket. This throws all of us into a tailspin, due to our innate desire to help the situation. Soon enough, an unexpected package may mysteriously arrive on a doorstep containing just what is needed.

Fortunately, we now have a vast network that can assist

with such urgent situations. We're able to send out a request, and someone around the country finds a solution. When time is of the essence; however, we don't always have the luxury of time for an item to be sent. One such story came from Mary Balagna, our coordinator in Forsyth, Illinois.

One day she was feeling a little down because a hospital was in need and she was out of blankets. Mary worried whether or not she would get the requested blankets. She remembered all the coordinators who shared how they prayed for blankets and received them. Mary said a prayer asking for help and subsequently went out to make a personal blanket delivery to a seriously ill girl's home. When Mary delivered the blanket, the girl's mother gave her a heartfelt hug and wouldn't let go—she was enormously thankful.

Mary returned home inspired and thought if she didn't have any blankets, she'd better get busy and make some. She began working on a baby quilt, when the phone rang. It was a member from a local quilt guild who had just received Mary's letter, sent to all the local guilds, letting them know about Project Linus and the need for blankets. The woman on the other end of the line was so excited that she could hardly speak. The guild had 49 blankets ready to present to Mary! *Coincidence?* Perhaps. I revert to the *Secret*—tell the Universe your needs, and it can't refuse. *Divine intervention?* I'll let you be the judge.

Sometimes the Project Linus angel shows herself in mysterious ways. We don't at the time realize what is going on, but afterwards there can be "a-ha" clarity. One such event happened when I was contacted about a Denver military service person who had been killed in the line of duty. His daughter, a little girl named Heaven, was to be our newest blanket recipient. Being a speed reader of my Blackberry device, I sometimes miss important details. I was told that a funeral would be held the Friday of Memorial Day weekend at 1pm. Since I had just delivered to a child of a deceased airman, I assumed this next blanket also needed to be taken to the chapel on the Air Force Academy Base in Colorado Springs. You can imagine my surprise when I showed up at the chapel and found wedding couples strategically posing for photos rather than the funereal, flag-bearing motorcycle honor guard I expected to see. The message had clearly stated the location of the funeral and burial site, were both in the Denver metro area- a full 60 miles away! Quite an important detail I had missed completely. I was definitely at the wrong site and would be too late to make the delivery as my holiday weekend plans had me continuing further away from Denver. I vowed to delivery as soon as was possible the next week.

I called the number listed for the church and asked if they could forward the blanket to Heaven on my behalf. The administrative person informed me that the date I'd been given was a week off. The serviceman was going to be buried the following Friday! I had a conflicting appointment during the funeral time so asked if I could drop a blanket off ahead of time at the church. No problem! When I arrived, the administrative assistant was warm and welcoming and shared with me that the family was currently in the next room making arrangements. Since I was unsure of the daughter's age, I'd brought two blankets—one with cute fuzzy chicks on it and the other with a more mature theme. As I offered to leave both blankets so the family could chose, the assistant noticed that the meeting was breaking up. She tenderly plucked up both blankets and took them to the room with the family. Less than a minute later, she emerged with glistening eyes and confided that the family was visibly moved when she offered the blanket for their child.

I heard a soft voice behind me say, "Is that the one?" The assistant nodded. I turned and found myself face to face with the brokenhearted grandmother of the deceased. She choked out a "thank you" and I held her in my arms. She was accompanied by her husband, the soldier's father. He too was visibly shaken and readily accepted my embrace of condolence. Although tongue-tied and groping for the right thing to say, during awkward moments such as this, the Project Linus blanket bridged the communication gap beautifully.

Sandy Wyatt, a coordinator from North Carolina, told of a time when a local church chose Project Linus as their monthly project. It is always an extra special treasure to receive blankets made by men, since this is such a rare occurrence. When Sandy received a blanket made by a fireman, with fire trucks on it, she couldn't bring herself to give it away just yet. Immediately after 9/11 occurred, 700 blankets were sent up to New York by several of the North Carolina chapters, and she included the firefighter's blanket. She later found out that the blanket was delivered to a child of one of the deceased NYFD firefighters.

After the FLDS (Fundamentalist Latter Day Saints) compound in Texas was raided, hundreds of children were removed. Judy Bell, the coordinator from the Fort Worth area, was told to bring as many blankets as she could. Judy has a robust personality and can talk "the color white off of milk," but she was particularly challenged when told that the blankets couldn't contain the color red or have any characters on them—such as Mickey Mouse, Dora or Thomas the Train—since they were deemed evil by the religious sect.

With the help of the Denton and Kaleen chapters, they were able to collect 465 blankets, practically vacuum-packing them into Judy's van. She couldn't even see out of her back window as she commandeered the two-hour drive with her husband Jess, a.k.a. "Sweet Thang." Security around the receiving site was extremely tight. The Bells were at the location for a total of ten minutes, while all the blankets were removed from their van. They were then told to immediately leave the premises. A few weeks later she received a letter saying there had been just enough blankets for each of the 465 children!

February 1998 brought with it a momentous event for the Denver chapter. The Mormon Church was celebrating their sesquicentennial, and in honor of that milestone, the local L.D.S. Stake wanted to hold a quilting bee to create 150 blankets to commemorate their church's anniversary. The saying "many hands make light work" certainly came into play that day. They created 225 blankets during that event! Helping hands were on deck from every age. Children acted as runners to get finished blankets from the quilt frame to the labeling table. Others manned the chalkboards to tally the new additions. There were three church buildings working simultaneously. A healthy rivalry developed as tallies were called in from the different locations.

My friend—and L.D.S. Stake community relations director—Margi shuttled me from building to building. We started in Parker, drove fifteen miles to Castle Rock, then finally another fifteen miles to Elizabeth. Little did we know that a new tradition was forming. From that day forward, we've had a Blanket Day the Saturday after Valentine's Day. This event has now grown into national "Make a Blanket Day." Many of that first year's blankets made their way over to Kazakhstan with a cardiology team from Denver's Children's Hospital.

A year later, one of the nurses, generous enough to donate her skills to that mission, came to our now-annual "Make a Blanket Day" activity and shared some of her experiences in Kazakhstan. We listened with captivated hearts and ears as she explained that each open-heart surgery generated about ten bags of trash. She painted a picture of the scenario, which happened in almost the identical fashion for each surgery. Throughout the operation, the surgery team placed the garbage bags outside the door for trash pickup. When the team finished the procedure, only two bags remained. The other eight bags were apparently taken and picked through to collect items for reuse—including gloves, syringes and other surgical items—supplies that the western world considers disposable. She explained that those scheduled for an operation were expected to bring their own supplies for the doctors to use—which included sutures, anesthesia, and bandages. If they didn't bring the supplies, those items simply weren't used for their procedure.

Her trip sounded so fascinating, and I felt a bit envious of the experience, until I learned that the esteemed medical team was presented with a coveted goat's head whenever they attended V.I.P. dinners. As guests, they were expected to savor this delicacy—eyeballs and all. My world-traveling sister-in-law Chris has a brilliant plan when faced with those situations—conveniently turn vegetarian!

The nurse also shared a story about one of the orphanages which received many of the Project Linus blankets. She set the stage for the story by reminding us that the children didn't have any of their own belongings. Even their underwear was communal. The day she and her group visited, the orphanage staff took the children outside to play. While the kids were out of sight, the nurses laid colorful Project Linus blankets on each of their beds. The look on the children's faces when they entered the room was one of bewilderment. It took a lot of explaining before the children understood that each of them was getting their very own blanket. Soon they were jumping around the room with pure joy. The blankets not only thrilled the orphans, but the bright colors and hip designs brightened the drab interior of the center. The orphanage staff was also delighted to be a part of bringing such happiness to the children.

Delivery styles vary from chapter to chapter. Blankets are bulky; there is no question about it. Anyone who has tried to deliver a couple dozen blankets knows this, let alone a couple hundred at a time. Originally, I delivered my blankets in large Hefty bags, which seemed to fit the bill nicely for strength, flexibility and cleanliness. This stopped abruptly; however, the day I was happily making a delivery and someone remarked that it looked as if I was bringing trash into the hospital. Of course it did, but I had never considered that before. I also realized that no one could see all the beautiful blankets contained in those obscure, bulky, black bags.

One solution came from a fan who attended our Polo in the Park events. He worked with mannequins that arrived from the factory in jumbo-sized, clear, plastic bags. Instead of throwing out the bags, he began to give them to me for blanket deliveries. The response was immediate. As I walked through the halls or waited for elevators with these colorful sacks of blankets, I'd hear lots of *ooh's* and *ah's* from passersby. A second unexpected benefit to the new bags was the recruitment of new Blanketeers. Many new blanket makers came on board simply after witnessing blanket deliveries!

Jean Jackson, a coordinator in Rhode Island, got her local U-Haul facility to donate moving boxes for her deliveries. Long Beach, California's coordinator Rebecca Hill delivered her local blankets in purple plastic laundry baskets stacked on foldable luggage carts. Some coordinators wrap colorful ribbons around the folded blanket and enclose a poem about Blanketeers. The delivery methods were as diverse as the chapters!

By our second anniversary, Project Linus had grown to 225 chapters in the United States, Canada and Australia.

CHAPTER 16

Straight to My Heart

*Life's most persistent and urgent question is,
'What are you doing for others?'*

- Martin Luther King, Jr.

While the eyes of the world focused on the Winter Olympics in Japan, one Nagano family concentrated on America. Their young son received a heart transplant from Denver's Children's Hospital. The little boy didn't speak English and had difficulty trying to figure out who all the poking and prodding strangers were. Unfortunately, the nursing staff didn't speak Japanese, but they did have one way to bring a smile to this young patient. They brought a Project Linus blanket to his room. It had an enormous crocheted cat on it. No translation was needed. The boy saw the blanket, broke into an ear-to-ear smile, and sweetly uttered "kitty" in Japanese. Like so many of the children who received blankets from Project Linus, each of them touched my heart in a different way. I have always been mesmerized by the unspoken universal language of a security blanket.

Meanwhile, expenses were an ongoing concern for everyone in the organization. Ginger had already donated an excess of $6,500 of our own funds, and we quickly needed to find a way to keep the organization afloat. In January of 1998, two years into Project Linus, Treasurer Cindy Guthrie sent out an announcement to all the chapters with some exciting news. A percentage of the donations sent to Headquarters would now be credited back to the chapter that received them. This helped us fund the national expenses and let the local chapters get reimbursed for some of their costs. It also gave them incentive to solicit more donations. All along, we were able to keep in compliance with the IRS rules by requiring receipts for all reimbursements—it was a win-win for everyone.

Another way we were able to assist the coordinators and Blanketeers with expenses was through the acquisition of a toll-free number. Back in the 90's, long-distance rates were still quite pricey, so it was an added bonus for all those trying to reach national headquarters on a regular basis.

Time felt as if it was moving fast, and in less than 30 months, Project Linus went from a mere fledgling idea to a nationwide (and multi-continental) nonprofit that was attracting a lot of media attention and press. Any time one of us was granted an award or news story, it benefitted the organization as a whole with upgraded credibility and additional Blanketeers.

In April, I became the recipient of the JCPenney Golden Rule Award. The award signifies the tradition of community service established by James Cash Penney in 1902, when he opened his first store, The Golden Rule. Mr. Penney told his associates and store managers to be guided by the Golden Rule, not only in the conduct of business, but as citizens of the community they served. A beautiful crystal flame trophy is the symbol of the Golden Rule Award. It is presented in recognition of outstanding volunteer service to an individual or group selected by a distinguished panel of civic leaders in a community-wide competition. In addition, award winners receive a $1,000 contribution to their nonprofit organization.

Receiving the Golden Rule Award advanced me to the national finals, and if chosen, Project Linus would receive an additional $10,000 donation, a sum that seemed like a million dollars at the time. Unfortunately, that didn't occur, but the $1,000 donation purchased a lot of blanket tags, and I was honored to be recognized for my work with Project Linus.

All of our chapters were run by individuals or a group of close friends or relatives. An exception to this rule was the San Diego chapter. Although we had a direct contact person, Project Linus was actually sponsored by the local chapter of Altrusa. The Altrusa National Organization was created in 1929, its purpose to provide community service by a network of executives and professionals in diversified career classifications. Altrusa International Foundation is dedicated to literacy, with a commitment to education and service. We felt abundantly blessed that they were sharing their time and talents with Project Linus. The San Diego chapter divided responsibilities between its members, which proved to be a terrific plan. No single person got buried by trying to do it all.

The San Diego chapter of the Altrusa National Organization holds an annual luncheon/fashion show to raise funds for their various service projects. In 1998, their program included a delightful luncheon followed by a talk I gave about Project Linus. There was a fashion show of garments from Draper's & Damon's of La Jolla, with Altrusa members as models, followed by a drawing and door prizes. This club certainly knows how to provide effective community service and have fun while doing it!

The Canadian chapters were rolling right along as well. Our Toronto chapter received lots of welcome surprises along the way. Not all donations to Project Linus came in the form of blankets. A head honcho at Scholastic Book Company, publisher of children's books, became a bit curious when he noticed one of his employees collecting blankets in her office. He decided to lend a hand to the effort after learning about Project Linus. Rona Kleiman, the Toronto coordinator, was delighted when she received 55 blankets from the group. Not only were the blankets lovely but they were accompanied by books and plush toys, courtesy of Scholastic Books.

Rona was also pleasantly surprised when she received quilt squares from two blind blanket makers. They had been taught how to make squares in class and wanted to share their handiwork with Project Linus. It was a true testament that the Blanketeers themselves are as varied as the blankets they make and the children who receive them.

Rona's daughter worked for the restaurant chain, Hooters. She and her fellow workers donned bikinis and did a car wash to raise money for her mother's chapter. They raised $186 and donated a desktop publishing computer program, thank you notes, a color ink cartridge and a gift certificate for yarn.

My mother, who was raised in Montreal, was thrilled when a chapter formed in her former province of Quebec. Guylaine Chalifour was our first bilingual chapter coordinator, and we were elated when she came on board. This useful skill allowed her to create the official French version of our brochure as well as set up a website for French-speaking Blanketeers.

The Women of the Moose is a club of wives of the Fraternal Order of Moose members. They often assist families who have lost a parent, and help the children with schooling and other essentials. Darlene Barber, the Hamilton, Ontario coordinator, was the lucky recipient of blankets made by this special club. Not only did they donate blankets, but they created blanket labels with the "Women of the Moose" printed on them. When Project Linus receives blankets with their makers' tags on them, we leave them in place and sew our tags side-by-side, so it shows our team effort.

In Mobile, Alabama, the Project Linus coordinator was chatting with a friend at a party. This gentleman was in the Mobile Optimist Club, a group that always looks for ways to help children. In fact, The Optimist Club built an entire children's playroom at the University of South Alabama Children's and Women's Hospital. This was the same facility where the coordinator Judi delivered blankets on a regular basis. After that conversation, the Mobile Optimists donated material to Project Linus, and one of their wives, who is an avid "garage saler," bought quite a bit of yarn. Judi then shared the yarn with R.S.V.P., a Retired Senior Volunteers Program that made beautiful blankets in striking combinations. It still amazes me how fervently people respond when they hear about opportunities to help others.

On April 8th, a series of 62 tornados touched down from Texas to the Mid-Atlantic States. Alabama was struck the hardest, with 34 deaths. When North Birmingham was hit by an F5 twister, local coordinator Elisa Atiyeh put out a call for help to her fellow coordinators around the country. The response was truly inspiring. Within a matter of days, almost 550 blankets were received. Those blankets went out to many children in need. Quite a few went to a high school that was destroyed near Elisa's home, where the students had to complete their school year outdoors. One senior lost both her parents and her sister in the tornadoes. When she graduated later that year, she did so with her Project Linus blanket in her arms.

CHAPTER
17

Peanuts

*If ever there is tomorrow when we're not together . . . there is
something you must always remember. You are braver than
you believe, stronger than you seem, and smarter than you
think. But the most important thing is, even if we're apart...
I'll always be with you.*

- Winnie the Pooh

By summertime, we had delivered over 40,000 blankets
and were about to be part of another national news
story. Traditionally, the Labor Day weekend cover
story for *Parade* magazine featured Jerry Lewis and the
Muscular Dystrophy telethon. This year was going to be
different. The magazine was doing a children's charity issue.
When Eddie Adams learned that Project Linus wasn't one
of the charities being considered, he used his clout and got
us included on the list, with an added surprise—we were
the cover shot! It just goes to show—it's not what you know,
but who you know! Not only was Eddie one of *Parade's* top
photographers, but the publisher of the magazine, Walter

Anderson, was well-acquainted with our efforts.

Two years prior, Eddie invited me to experience a unique photographic event he held at his pastoral farm in Jeffersonville, New York, just a few miles outside of the infamous Woodstock. The intense, four-day event, called the Eddie Adams Workshop (a.k.a. Barnstorm), is a gathering of the top photography professionals along with 100 carefully-selected students. The photography workshop is tuition-free, and the 100 students are chosen based on the merit of their portfolios. Famous figures throughout the photography world participate as speakers, editors, and publishers, giving the amateur photographers the opportunity to rub shoulders with the likes of Eddie, Gordon Parks, Joe Rosenthal (Iwo Jima), Nick Ut, Carl Mydens, Peter Jennings, Kathleen Kennedy Cuomo, Sam Garcia, Walter Anderson, and a laundry list of other notables in the photography world.

Along with being a magical gathering of top talents, this workshop was also Eddie and his wife Alyssa's way to give the new generation of photographers their first break. Eddie was proud that his images were an inspiration for Project Linus and wanted me to be his special guest. I asked Tina to join me on this adventure, since I didn't know what to expect. It turned out to be a weekend that added to our awareness of a different side to the media. The two of us experienced a sort of "media spiritual awakening." Although I had been a journalism major and a huge fan of photojournalism, I'd never really made the connection of what it takes to bring it all together so that when we open our morning paper, the story and picture jump out and grab our hearts and minds. Needless to say, it was an event that I thoroughly enjoyed, and for ten straight years, I returned to volunteer my services.

As for the *Parade* photo shoot, we stood a serious chance of not getting on the cover, or even featured as an inside story, due to one factor that was entirely out of our control—weather. In general, Colorado has a highly predictable, late-summer weather pattern. It is typically warm and dry during the day, but often in the afternoon, we experience brief thunder showers. It is a very rare occurrence that the Denver area receives morning rain. Unfortunately, the weather happened to be uncharacteristic during the time Eddie scheduled the shoot. Eddie spent the prior night of August 3rd at our rain-drenched ranch. We were then scheduled for an early photo shoot the following morning. The last thing he said before retiring to the guest room was that he hoped the weather would clear up.

At 6:30 the next morning, it was cloudy but dry. The living room was a flurry of activity. My friends, who were mothers, signed model releases while their children played. Just as Eddie started with the first shots, the rain resumed. We waited several hours, until there was a mild break in the rain, and the sun gave a feeble attempt to shine. We dashed out with one of the "models" Katrina Frakes, the 7-year-old daughter of my St. Matthew's Netcasters buddy, Melissa, for a quick shoot by the barn before the foul weather resumed. Eddie released everyone once the National Weather Service forecasted more of the same for the rest of the day.

Four children remained—awaiting rides—when the rain subsided briefly and it brightened outside. Eddie again took advantage of the short-lived respite and ended up with a quality shoot, despite the poor conditions. What a professional he was throughout this trying and nerve-wracking ordeal! We had no way to know for certain, however, what these shots would look like since this was before the days of digital photography. I drove Eddie back to Parker so he could put the rolls of film in a UPS envelope and overnight it back to his editors at *Parade*. We hoped there would be at least one image that could be used. I had to wait until the following Sunday morning to see what would become of our efforts.

The *Mike and Maty* experience taught us that national exposure can produce a media onslaught. Again, an all-hands-on-deck shout for help went out in anticipation of the phone calls we expected to receive. Knowing that the paper would start to reach people around 6 a.m. on the East Coast, I woke up extra early and prepared the coffee table for the task at hand: one fully-charged cordless phone. *Check*. One empty notebook with a variety of pens. *Check*. A list of current chapters and contact info. *Check*. Excited, but still tired from the wee morning hour, I drifted off to sleep on the couch.

A couple hours later, I woke with a jolt. Why was the phone still quiet? Had *Parade* changed their minds and decided not to include us? I raced up the driveway with phone in hand—in case someone called while I was out of the house—to pick up my own copy of the paper. Hastily, I pulled the newspaper out of its protective plastic sleeve. I felt like Charlie Bucket as he nervously unwrapped a chocolate bar, hoping to find the Willie Wonka golden ticket. Indeed, there was a striking image of Katrina on the cover looking out at the world, with her reflective brown eyes and thick shock of dark hair peeking out from underneath a teal-colored, knitted blanket in front of the blue and green barn doors, painted in our polo team colors. The inside story was entitled "How You Can Help a Child." Project Linus got a second boost by leading the stories along with another picture that included me with my friend Kyle Wagner's two daughters, Liza and Maggie. Kai, my friend Melanie's 7-year-old son, also joined us in the picture. I took the paper back to the house and inspected the *Parade* magazine section. There, on page 4, was our photo, along with the article. *So, why weren't people calling?*

Other efforts were also featured in the article. One of the highlighted individuals was Mark Donegan of Portland, Oregon, who assisted a student from a difficult home environment with a scholarship. She was able to attend a college preparatory school that her family couldn't afford. Another individual was Fran Janick of Sterling Heights, Michigan, who gathered toys, books, games and puzzles to give as gifts to the disabled students in her community. Eloise Wardell of Savannah, Georgia, was yet another, who provided love and nurturing to seriously ill or premature babies, as well as those who'd been abused, abandoned or whose parents could not care for them. Her nonprofit was appropriately named Open Arms. Marc Brown, of Indianapolis, helped foster kids get proper luggage for carrying their belongings from one home to another, through the effort he founded, called FosterCare Luggage.

It wasn't until I got to the section containing contact information for Project Linus that I found my answer. Our mailing address and website were listed, but no phone number. What at first seemed like an immense oversight, truly ended up being a blessing. We soon learned that the Project Linus website was visited over 14,000 times! People were immediately able to locate chapters and get answers to the most commonly-asked questions. We received email from individuals who didn't have chapters near them, from others who were interested in starting chapters, and those who asked for blanket patterns. By Wednesday, the letters started pouring in. Our national assistant Betsy, and a few treasured others, processed over 5,100 pieces of mail in a matter of weeks. Betsy and I split the email, and I also handled the phone calls that resulted from the website's phone number listing.

Needless to say, we were delightfully frazzled people. It was becoming increasingly evident that, with this level of activity, we desperately needed to hire an office manager. The problem was that the monetary donations weren't coming in to support this staff position. Out of the more than 5,000 pieces of mail we received, less than $250 was enclosed. Most people didn't even include a self-addressed, stamped envelope or a simple stamp. It didn't take an accountant to figure out that the expenses going out far outpaced the funds coming in. Postage, printing of brochures, long-distance calls and office supplies were bleeding our limited financial resources dry. Without professional help, we were feeling more drained with each passing day.

Fundraising, the one thing I had shied away from since the beginning of Project Linus, was now my main focus. The fact of life for any business not receiving regular contributions of materials is that fundraising must happen—or a sponsor must be found. Soliciting funds became a necessary role for the survival of Project Linus. We decided to reach out for help and talk with our coordinators. We asked them to put on their thinking caps. We needed new tactics to fund our efforts. We requested that they contact their employers, since many businesses offer incentives to employees who participate in charities.

Even the Blanketeers got involved in our fundraising efforts. Nina Delaune of Baton Rouge, Louisiana, approached her employer, Glaxo-Wellcome Pharmaceuticals. They kindly donated $500. Craig Connolly, our webmaster, connected us to Amazon for their fundraising program. For every Amazon consumer who purchased through a link on our website, we received a small percentage of that purchase price.

I also started to put time into grant writing. Despite my journalism degree, I didn't have experience in this area. Successful grants have to be written in very specific ways, and I quickly got up to speed on the requirements. I applied for all levels of grant funding—locally, nationally, and internationally. Funds trickled in, but nothing as large as the mother lode needed to hire an employee.

I learned that the Junior League might be an excellent resource for help, yet when I spoke with the Denver Chapter, they informed me that the grant writers have to be financially compensated. There were two ways of doing this. One option was to pay the grant writer for the actual hours worked, although we didn't have funds to hire someone. The second was to pay the grant writer a percentage of what was raised on our behalf. This second option felt like a moral dilemma. I know when I donate money to a charity, I want as much as possible to go to that charity. Even though I understood that the grant writer would be performing a valuable job, I felt conflicted.

The same was true for a philanthropist club called the Denver Active 2030 Children's Foundation. They were the male equivalent to the Junior League, with the slogan, "A man never stands so tall as when kneeling to help a child."

They hold large-scale fundraisers, including an annual polo tournament. The members were thrilled to have Ginger make guest appearances at their events and seemed to love Project Linus. They insisted that Project Linus would be a natural fit for their goal to help children's organizations. The club grants over $500,000 to more than 50 children's organizations each year, yet Project Linus never saw a penny. We were in a Catch 22. We had no funds to hire a grant writer, and without a grant writer, we couldn't get funds.

It seemed we needed a miracle for Project Linus to continue. *If only Oprah would invite us on her show.* She was such a wise and wealthy woman. Surely, she would see the good we were doing for children of every race, creed and color. Surely, she would help us. I asked everyone I knew to start a letter-writing campaign to Oprah and let her know how Project Linus had personally affected their lives, the lives of their loved ones, and how much her viewers needed to hear about our efforts.

Meanwhile, publicity continued to flow for Project Linus. An article on our efforts came out in *Crafts & Things*, followed by another mega opportunity—a two-page spread in *People Magazine*. My hair dresser, Kevin Carter, kindly agreed to come out to the ranch to expertly do my hair and makeup for this shoot. Ten years prior, I had appeared in an article in *People* about Ginger as his sidekick. Now he was appearing as mine! Again, a whole new wave of volunteers emerged from that article and continued to roll in for many months. The best thing about print media is that it stays around for a long time. People will clip an article and act on it years later. Magazines float around doctor's offices, hair salons, and homes for months and sometimes even years. With television, it is so easy to miss a significant segment when the doorbell rings, a phone call comes in, or the baby needs changing. In two years, we had received a lot of exciting press and publicity, and the best part—it hadn't cost us much more than postage required to send out a press release.

One of my favorite outcomes from the *People* article was that United Media was finally ready to talk specifics about the Linus image. I flew to their New York corporate offices, and we came to an agreement. Project Linus would be allowed limited use of the image—finally! Linus could be used strictly on our blanket tags and webpage for a two-year period. After that time, they would reevaluate and decide if they wanted to continue the partnership. We had done it! That loveable little character would now be officially associated with our effort.

Another exciting media opportunity occurred when coordinators were given a "heads up" to set their VCR's to record the Leeza show, which aired on NBC that December. Leeza Gibbons delivered 50 Project Linus blankets, donated courtesy of Mary Jane Napollilo of Rancho Palos Verdes, California. Leeza was so impressed with Project Linus that she decided to form one of our newest chapters—Project Linus Hollywood! This chapter was run by the staff of the Leeza Show at Paramount Studios.

On good days, I referred to the Project Linus effort as blossoming. On tougher days, it was mushrooming—continuing to grow like fungus in the dark. Lew Wyatt, husband of Reidsville, North Carolina coordinator Sandy, referred to the growth of interest in Project Linus as "kudzu"—a quick-growing southern weed. Perhaps another analogy would have been bamboo. It kept growing and growing. Despite our financial woes, Project Linus was strong.

The stress of so much success was starting to affect our all-volunteer headquarters staff. By December, our special assistant Laurie Huffman had to resign for health reasons. With her steadfast diligence, she had been an immense aid to our effort. With classic dedication to Project Linus, Laurie didn't leave us in the lurch. Laurie found a fabulous replacement, Gini Warren. Gini had terrific administrative skills and actually—*gasp*—enjoyed doing paperwork! We were delighted to have Gini join the Project Linus family. Another legacy Laurie left us was her daughter, Angie Ulibarrie, who then became our Northern Utah coordinator.

A second health crisis struck Project Linus' first Blanketeer, Hooker and Board Secretary, Shirley Harden. She was diagnosed with breast cancer. During our fall taping of a segment for the national television show *Simply Quilts,* on the Home and Garden Network, she asked us all to pray that her quickly shedding hair would stay attached until the end of the shoot, due to the side effects from her chemotherapy regime. Her hair had become so fragile that a simple puff of air could blow it away. No one who watched that show knew that Shirley was sick. She was such a good sport. Despite her own personal battles with this insipid disease, Shirley still went to the hospital with me to make deliveries. When she walked into the hospital room with a bandana covering her bald head, Shirley made an instant connection with the pediatric oncology patients. She was someone they were able to relate to as one of their own, and they immediately clicked like long-lost friends.

Although Shirley eventually succumbed to cancer, after a five-year battle, she continued on as an active volunteer for as long as her health allowed. Shirley made a difference in thousands of children's lives through her blankets and the work she did with Project Linus. She inspired many of us to get tested for the national bone marrow donor registry. I encourage everyone to consider participation in this noble cause. It's free, it's easy, and it can save lives. Additionally, it's a magnificent tribute to an unforgettable person.

CHAPTER 18

Spanning the Globe

Don't ask yourself what the world needs, ask yourself what makes you come alive. And then go and do that. Because what the world needs is people who are alive.

- Howard Thurman

In 1999, Project Linus began making its presence known globally—from Africa, to Europe, to Russia, to South America, to Australia, to Asia. My year started with a trip to South Africa. Ginger and I were looking for horse property to acquire. As an English citizen, he'd experienced some complications with U.S. Immigration in prior decades. Annually, he was required to go back to England and get his passport stamped with a new H1 work visa. With each passing year, it took longer and longer for that process to be completed. What started as a one-day wait became, by 1998, an extremely lengthy stay—Ginger was forced to remain in England for an entire month to get his visa! I tried to get him to view this time as an opportunity. He was able to spend time with this family, which included a gorgeous granddaughter named Zara, and watch cricket test matches galore. Instead, he was miserable not being at home, surrounded by his animals, and he had deep-seated fears that one day the U.S. would simply refuse him reentry altogether. All his hard work on the ranch and the building of a polo community would be for naught. The thought of that greatly distressed him.

South Africa seemed to be a great alternative to the States. It is an Anglo-friendly country with many of his favorite grocery items regularly stocked at its local markets. PG Tips tea, Wheatabix cereal, HP Sauce, Maltesers, Coleman's mustard, Horlicks malted milk, jam teacakes and treacle were in steady supply on the southern tip of the African continent. Conversely, to get these items in the U.S., I had to pay premium prices at specialty shops. Like many ex-patriots, a trip to the U.K. often resulted in an extra suitcase jammed with comfort foods. There was also a very active polo scene in South Africa that didn't exist in the Denver area. On this trip, we located a 60-acre ranch in Kwa Zulu Natal which we purchased. It was just a couple miles from a polo field, and plans were put in motion for him to move there.

Ginger and I had been growing apart over the years, and the last thing I wanted to do was relocate our troubled relationship halfway around the globe. Moving would take me away from my friends, family, Project Linus, and into the heart of a very dodgy living situation—at home as well as in the surrounding neighborhoods. Violence against white landowners was not uncommon, and at that time, South Africa was reporting that one out of every three women was victim to rape. Those kinds of odds were not anything I was interested in challenging. If things had been looking up in our relationship, I might have considered moving there, especially since I've always wanted to live in a foreign country. At the time, however it didn't seem to be in the cards.

During that trip, I brought a dozen blankets with me, and we hand-delivered them to children with AIDS in Cape Town. The Nazareth House orphanage cared for about 40 children and was very pleased to receive the blankets. A list of Blanketeers' names and addresses was included with the delivery. Within two weeks, calls came in to Headquarters from joyous Blanketeers sharing that they had received lovely thank you letters from South Africa.

⁓

Soon, other opportunities to spread Project Linus in Africa, and beyond, were brought to our attention. As a volunteer with the Rattlesnake Fire Department since 1995, I have served in roles as firefighter, EMT and community relations coordinator. A fellow firefighter, Bryan Pippitt, told me that his parents were going to Zimbabwe on a humanitarian mission. They took a dozen blankets with them and were delighted at the prospect of sharing Project Linus with this troubled nation's children.

Karin Baudouin became the chapter coordinator in Mexico City. Although Karin was originally from California, she and her husband had moved to Mexico eight years earlier. She was a member of a local Junior League chapter and as an insider, looked forward to employing their support for her Project Linus chapter.

Long Island's Elizabeth Cassidy assisted with a local effort to help the people of Colombia after a devastating earthquake.

She contributed 75 blankets to the effort. Moving that many blankets in your car is a challenge. Trying to get them to another continent is an even bigger one. We didn't have the funding to ship them internationally, so when blankets were transported to other parts of the world, they usually got there in someone's luggage or found a spot in a cargo container of medical or relief supplies with an already-existing effort.

Other countries whose children received blankets during this time included England, Australia, Guatemala, Honduras, Japan and Kazakhstan. Being able to share blankets with disaster and war-torn areas was made possible by partnering with established relief efforts. Somehow, we always found a way to reach the children, despite our lack of funds.

A frequent question I receive is whether Project Linus teams up with The American Red Cross. That would have been a natural collaboration, since we serve many of the same people. I approached them on several occasions and was flatly told that although they do need blankets, they are only interested in identical ones, like those provided by an airline. We specialize in unique, handmade blankets, so it doesn't seem that we are a fit after all.

I started listening to radio personality Dr. Laura Schlessinger back in the mid-1980's while I was living in Los Angeles. It was impressive how quickly she could get to the heart of a problem and come up with immediate, snappy solutions. I heard that Dr. Laura's foundation aided children, so I decided to contact her. I sent a grant request, and they, in turn, asked us for 500 blankets. They were working on a powerful project, filling 500 "My Stuff" duffel bags for traumatized children. Included in each bag were toiletries, books, toys and other comfort items.

When they heard about Project Linus, they immediately recognized that each bag needed to contain a security blanket! We put the word out to the coordinators that we needed 500 blankets, and our goal was swiftly met. The next hurdle was to determine how to get these 500 blankets to Dr. Laura's hometown. Although Dr. Laura's foundation offered us the use of its shipping account, it would have cost them a lot of money. Our frugality wouldn't allow us to waste any organization's hard-earned money if there was another option.

Many of the blankets came from chapters that were in relative proximity to Dr. Laura's San Fernando Valley. California coordinators Elysse Johnston of Valencia and Katie Duran of Arcardia were quick to help, and Janet Eubank, a coordinator from clear across the country in the Norfolk & Virginia Beach area, sent some of her chapter blankets as well. We were also able to send blankets from the Denver area via a friend's moving company, Bailey's Allied Van Lines. They had a truck that delivered to the L.A. area weekly. To compensate Project Linus for all its efforts, the foundation contributed a copy machine to assist Betsy with administrative work. This partnership was a win-win for everyone.

CHAPTER
19

Be Still My Beating Heart

I believe that every human mind feels
pleasure in doing good to another.

- Thomas Jefferson

Although a lot of work was going on around the country and the world, we were to soon learn just how important the gift of a security blanket could be in our own backyard. April 20, 1999 will be a date to live in infamy in Colorado and put the name of our state flower—which also happened to be that of a high school southwest of Denver—on the lips of every American. We found ourselves trying to help heal our own community. Keeping up with Project Linus' national needs became a secondary focus for a few weeks to follow.

On April 28th, Betsy sent a note to our coordinators explaining why we had fallen behind over the past couple of weeks. It read:

Dear Fellow Coordinators,

As most of you know, Project Linus Headquarters is in the same community as Columbine High School. We have all been very saddened by the event of last Tuesday, as we know you have. After receiving many calls and emails from chapters all over and even some messages asking, "Where are you guys?" I felt like a quick note may help. I, no, we all appreciate all your concerns and prayers. It has meant a lot to know that you care. I would like to share with you how this has hit home for me...and how Project Linus has helped.

First, being a mom of a high school student, this hit very close to home from the minute I first heard about the shooting. There was even a bomb found at my daughter's high school that very same morning. It turned out to be a fake bomb and a very bad senior prank. It wasn't until a church service on Wednesday night (day after shooting), did we realize that we know two of the victims and some of the children and a teacher who survived. Both children and their families attend my church. I was honored to be asked to serve as an usher at one of their funerals. And later this morning, I will be attending another funeral along with my oldest daughter. Please believe all the wonderful things you hear about these two children. They were truly a blessing to all of us and both with truly be missed.

Now, for a little good news. On Tuesday night, the 20th, Karen took 25 PL blankets down to one of the local churches (which was having a community worship service). The wonderful ladies at the church were very kind and thanked Karen but said that the students they had at their church were teenagers, not six year olds; most of them football players, cheerleaders and upper classmen. They wouldn't want blankets. Karen asked the women to please leave the blankets in the counseling room and if the kids wanted them, great. If not, we would come back and pick them up. Well, the next morning, the nice lady called back. She had done what Karen had asked and then had left the room because the kids and counselors wanted to be alone. When she walked by a short time later, something caught her eye. She looked back into the room and there were 25 kids sitting around in a circle, all with a blanket wrapped around them. Then more kids came and the church went out and bought 20 more blankets. The adults were overwhelmed to see the kids and their blankets. Could we please bring more? Soon, the same thing happened at other churches in that area. We even had stories of how some kids who got a blanket on Tuesday night, as of Thursday, had still not changed their clothes, or taken baths and parents were worried because they had not eaten. The only thing the kids seemed to be able to do was hang onto their blankets. From home to school to church and back home, they held onto those blankets. I know it is the love and prayers of all the PL volunteers that allow those blankets to give so much comfort.

We started running out of blankets—what to do? Three churches in Parker, Elizabeth and Castle Rock have held annual quilting bees the past three years for PL. The last one was in February. Though they made 566 blankets that day, I knew that they still had leftover supplies as well as blankets that were not quite finished. Perhaps they had finished those blankets and we could use the supplies. Well, not too long after my first call went out, I received a call. Not only did they have a few blankets ready to go but they were going to work all weekend and make us some more blankets for the Columbine kids. They made close to 150 blankets Friday night and Saturday with many donations from local businesses. But more were needed.

Then another amazing thing happened, at least it was amazing to me. People started asking how they could help and kids who had received blankets wanted to make some to help other students! Could we please come and help set up a quilting bee for these kids? Sunday night, we went to meet with the church which offered to host the bee. It was obvious these ladies meant well but emotionally, they could not handle the task. So, the ladies from Parker offered to jump right in and set it all up. And they did. Tuesday morning, the quilting bee began. People from all over the community showed up to help. Fabric, batting, yarn, thread and food started to arrive. Volunteers to piece, to sort, sew and tie were there. Soon Columbine and the other schools arrived. Some to help—others for a blanket. It was truly a wonderful sight. Today, we will continue the quilting bee.

Again, I would like to thank you for your patience with us. As you can see, we have been unable to deal with requests for labels, general information and chapter questions. We hope that you all understand that the Columbine community and our families must come first and that we will try to get back to business in a few days. Thank you all for your support and we ask that you keep praying for us, long after the press and others go away. It will take a long time for these children to heal. I thank you all for letting me write this, because it helped me. I thank you all again and again.

Betsy

The *Rocky Mountain News* and *Denver Post* were instrumental in alerting the community about this effort. Everyone who wanted to lend a hand was welcome. Three separate quilting bees were held—three days in Littleton (the Columbine neighborhood), one day in Golden, and two days in Colorado Springs. I heard over and over from participants how much being able to help, in a tangible, hands-on fashion, actually supported them with their healing process. Simply writing a check doesn't give us the same level of relief. Some families took their children to fabric stores to have them pick out fabric to donate. Other Columbine students brought in their school tee-shirt and requested to have their quilt made out of that. Volunteers were only too happy to comply. Memorial blankets were made and presented to each of the families who lost a student. I was able to personally deliver specially-made blankets to the family of the slain teacher. It was surreal to have to pass the police standing in front of their home in order to make the delivery.

So many people came out of the woodwork to assist. I requested food donations from a local grocery story, Albertsons, to help sustain our hundreds of volunteers. They handed me a grocery cart and said to take what we needed. Bagels, cream cheese, juice, milk, bread, peanut butter and jelly, and fruit all helped to keep the volunteers sustained. Other people brought platters of food from their homes. Donated pizza deliveries arrived by the dozen, six-foot long subs, baked goods, and bottled water continued to arrive in a steady flow throughout this effort.

Everyone did what they could to make the event a success. It would be impossible to name all the people who contributed, but you know who you are and we thank you! In a short time, we had enough blankets to give each of the 1,600 Columbine students a Project Linus blanket. Over the years, I have met several recipient students who, to this day, still treasure their blanket.

The first victim of the shooting was a girl named Rachel Scott. She left quite a legacy behind her with prophetic journals and a desire to start a chain reaction of kindness and compassion. Her father and many of her loved ones continue to carry this message to schools all over the country in the form of *Rachel's Challenge*. In a nutshell, her recipe to eliminate prejudice was built on five challenges each of us can choose to take:

1. Only look for the best in others.
2. Dare to dream.
3. Choose positive influences.
4. Choose kind words—little acts of kindness can produce HUGE results.
5. Tell the people in your life how you feel about them.

There were many contributing factors that transformed the two shooters from straight A students to maniacal monsters who could inflict such carnage on their community. Books have been written on the subject so—as an untrained person in the field of psychiatry—I'm not going to try to dissect their actions. But I can say with certainty that if they had applied the principles of *Rachel's Challenge* to their lives, such a horrific event would probably not have occurred.

There are many parallels between Rachel's life and that of Anne Frank's. Both died way too young, they each left important writings, and each of them wanted to make a positive difference in the world. I believe, in their very short lives, they accomplished that goal and more.

CHAPTER 20

After the Rain has Fallen

Being involved in the well being and advancement of one's
own community is a most natural thing to do.

- Clarence Clemons

As the Columbine event began to slowly fade away, normalcy started to creep its way back into our lives. More publicity and growth sprang forth. This time, the *Simply Quilts* show from the Home and Garden Network replayed the prior year's Project Linus segment and an article about our effort ran in *Reader's Digest*. Do you know how long some people hold on to their *Reader's Digest* copies? For years! And that would bring years of renewed interest to our effort as fresh readers eyed the article. Many new Blanketeers got involved. The website was viewed by its 100,000th visitor and continued to be an excellent source of information for potential Blanketeers and coordinators.

We'd spent much of what remained of the spring making a Project Linus dream come true—the fruition of our first National Conference which was held in June. Since this was our first attempt to hold a national event, it was a real blessing that we only had around 20 attendees. They were supportive "guinea pigs" and helped us set some of the traditions that continue at our conferences today. Coordinators arrived from as far away as Canada for this premier event, bringing along with them their great attitudes and a desire to get to know the organization and each other better.

We planned a variety of "short and sweet" discussions that were suggested ahead of time by coordinators. They included finding Blanketeers, packaging and delivery ideas, public relations, organizational skills, speaking before groups, administration, blanketing techniques and scrapbooking for a historical account of their chapters. We also started a fun show-and-tell-type tradition where coordinators were invited to share information about their chapters. This ended up being an annual favorite. We were all curious to see what each other was doing.

The conference began at noon at a hotel in the south Denver area. There was an introduction of officers, discussions and plenty of time to network. That evening we went across the street to a dinner theatre and enjoyed the production, *The Music Man.*

Saturday morning brought more discussions, followed by a double-decker bus ride to the Celestial Seasoning tea factory in Boulder, where we enjoyed a community luncheon and tour. There was free time, and in the afternoon, weather permitted a poolside barbeque at the hotel. We enjoyed a Sunday morning brunch together with more sharing time, and then the attendees departed to their respective hometowns. Not only had new friendships been forged, but solidarity was felt amongst the group.

We, the Headquarters staff, let out a collective sigh of relief. Originally, we thought that Denver would be the optimal location for our National Conference, since it is centrally located to most of the country and it was the hometown for the Headquarters staff and our families (offering extra helping hands). One thing we had not anticipated though was how much the altitude was going to affect the attendees. Most of the out-of-towners were flatlanders, and many were not in optimal physical shape. Fortunately, besides the walk to the dinner theatre, there wasn't much physical exertion required of the attendees. Even with that, however, there definitely was a lot of huffing and puffing going on as well as some fatigue, light-headedness, an occasional nosebleed and headache, and even some edema (swelling of the extremities). The last thing we wanted to do was to put anyone's health at risk. We learned we would have to minimize exertion if we wanted to continue conferences in the Mile High City. Ultimately, we acknowledged that we had successfully pulled off our first conference—and it was good.

That fall, one of our most vivacious coordinators, JoAnn Holley of Northern Virginia, got tickets to the *Rosie O'Donnell Show*. She cleverly made tee-shirts stating "Hey Rosie, Ask Me about Project Linus!" She and a friend arrived at six in the morning and were second and third in line. They waited three hours before the studio let the audience into the building. The shirt, combined with her spirited personality, must have caught the eye and ear of the warm-up personality, Joey Kola. He invited JoAnn and her friend to follow him. They entered the building, thrilled at the thought that he might let them use the bathroom. After all, a girl has her priorities straight after three hours of coffee drinking!

It wasn't until they were in an elevator that he introduced himself as not only the warm-up guy but also the person who peruses the audience line for someone he can introduce to Rosie during the show. The person for that day was JoAnn! She was given a heads-up that, time permitting, Rosie might ask her a few questions. JoAnn admits that she can talk about Project Linus for 24 hours a day, so when Rosie asked her to come up, JoAnn took to the stage like a duck to water. The rapport between Rosie and JoAnn was like two longtime friends. JoAnn was a natural and gave a beautiful plug for Project Linus. Without any forewarning, the trickle-down effect of her appearance lit up coordinator phone lines across the country—especially after the show flashed the Project Linus web address. With each of these endorsements, we were gaining more and more clout throughout the craft world and with the public at large.

By late fall, news surfaced that the creator of Linus, Charles Schulz, was in a personal battle with cancer. It sparked a tradition that the coordinators still do to this day. We had a card shower for Mr. Schulz. This involved sending cards and letters of well wishes to him from all over the country. Through our LinusCoords, an email distribution list for coordinators, anytime we have a volunteer who has a significant birthday, is sick or has had a family member die, the cards come out and dozens of notes are sent to that person or their family. I witnessed the place of honor my Blanketeer extraordinaire Teri Otsuki had for her cards. While visiting her tiny shared space in the nursing home after her 85th birthday, she offered me a seat on her bed. She then gingerly pulled out a special box that contained these precious notes. Teri was so excited that people from all over the country had sent her well wishes, and she truly treasured each and every one of them.

Project Linus continued to grow exponentially. By March, we delivered 75,000 blankets, 90,000 by June and 140,000 by our fourth year birthday in December! A date was set for our Second Annual Conference, and we were rolling right along. So many wonderful things were happening, and I was elated to witness the beautiful team effort and observe the personal growth of coordinators and Blanketeers alike.

CHAPTER
21

Center Stage

I trust that everything happens for a reason,
even when we're not wise enough to see it.

- Oprah Winfrey

Have you ever had one of those years that was a bit of a blur? Perhaps you had a new baby in the house. Or someone you loved just passed away which threw you into a tailspin. Or maybe you were juggling a full-time job, raising a family, and working towards a degree. The year 2000 was that blurry year for me.

Ginger and I were in the final stretch of getting a divorce, and I had to set my sights on a new future—one that wouldn't include him. Anyone who has been through a divorce knows the "bittersweetness" of this life-changing event. Even though for years things had been steadily spiraling downward, I optimistically greeted each morning with the hope that perhaps this was the day everything would be different. That dream never did come to fruition. So it was with some sadness—along with some relief—that I greeted the New Year. Along with those mixed feelings was mounting excitement for the many opportunities which might reveal themselves. Looking ahead, the biggest challenge would be figuring out how to support myself. I either had to develop a paid position for myself with Project Linus—which would require funding—or I needed to put my energies into new directions to keep my head above water.

The divorce with Ginger was finalized in February. Although I was thrilled for this opportunity and a new beginning, there was yet another looming issue high on my list of priorities. In order to get Ginger the needed funds to move him, his horses and our dogs to South Africa, we had to pull the last seven years' earned equity from the Parker ranch. Ginger liquidated his accounts and shifted them to a tax-free, off-shore account. He promised to reimburse me for the house funds with his upcoming royalty checks. Although I had personally witnessed him leave debt after debt in his wake, I was eager to have him move on. I just hoped this time he would be true to his word. Due to distance and country lines, there wouldn't be any way to collect regularly-scheduled alimony payments from him, despite our ten-year marriage. The question remained: *How was I going to support myself?*

I put the ranch on the market with the hope that it would be a good fit for someone. Perhaps a Ginger Baker fan would find it a sentimental investment. As much as I love being out in the country, I'm really a suburbs girl and feel most comfortable with close-by neighbors and a smaller piece of property to maintain. Ten acres was a rather large slice of heaven to keep groomed and much more space than I actually needed for myself, my cat and some goldfish. I optimistically hoped that the property would sell quickly so that I could downsize to a cozy home closer to town. Selling would also give me some much-needed funds to keep going. Until the house sold, I had a sizeable monthly mortgage payment to fulfill as well as normal living expenses—including healthcare, upkeep of the ranch and Project Linus.

It is said that you never work harder than when you work for yourself. That saying certainly applied to my involvement with Project Linus. My original, simple vision had turned into much more than a full-time job. There was never "off-time" when I could just clock out and shelve work for awhile. I wasn't accruing sick time or vacation time, a pension, or any other benefits that could help me financially.

Early in the spring, I received the call I'd been hoping for since the first days of Project Linus. It was from one of the Harpo producers at *Oprah*. They wanted an interview to see if Project Linus might be a good fit for Oprah's show. I was absolutely giddy sharing some of the heartrending stories experienced by Project Linus. A few weeks later, another call came with yet another interview. Interview by interview, we were working our way up the chain of command.

I had my eyes set on the brass ring—to have Project Linus featured on Oprah's show. Finally, I got the call! Yes, indeed, they wanted to feature us. This was the answer to our prayers and just in the nick of time. It appeared that we were going to be saved and Oprah was going to be our knight in shining armor! We'd be able to evolve as we'd envisioned, transporting Project Linus to the next stage of growth. Maybe we would have real office space instead of working from our kitchen tables. Maybe we could stop fretting about how to cover our ongoing expenses. Better yet, paid staff could finally be hired who would be able to turn the key at night, lock the doors behind them, and get on with their lives. At last, I could be compensated for my role at the helm of the Project Linus ship. What a much nicer vision than being plagued with this 24-7 need to catch up. Oh, the dreaming was divine!

On the Friday before Easter, a camera crew came out to the ranch for some "on the scene" footage. They set up in my living room and interviewed several of us from the Headquarters staff. They also wanted to capture a Project Linus delivery. The Marketing Department at Children's Hospital in Denver was thrilled when I shared the news that the Oprah crew wanted to come and video some patients as they received blankets. Unfortunately, the timing wasn't optimal. It was a holiday weekend and, as with most holidays, the staff tries to release any patient who is well enough to celebrate at home with their families. The hospital was a virtual ghost town compared to its typical daily beehive of activity.

We were warmly greeted at the hospital by a public relations staff member. Sadly, she hadn't done her homework, and precious time was wasted as we tried to locate likely recipients. It must have been a comical scene with a video crew and a phalanx of volunteers tugging on the handles of overloaded red wagons as we marched up and down the deserted halls. Most of the rooms were empty, and the occupants we did find were very ill children. An added hurdle we encountered was the time—it was getting close to 8 p.m. Many of the children were already asleep.

Once a perspective child was located, the P.R. staffer went in and talked with the family. If the family wasn't there, the child couldn't be videotaped, since releases had to be signed by a guardian. Some of the patients and their families were strictly Spanish-speaking. This posed an added difficulty, because we didn't have an interpreter in our midst. We did have two things going for us, though—the first, we were taping for the *Oprah* show; and the other, we came bearing gifts. Finally, the crew was able to obtain the footage, and we waited to hear back from the producers of the show.

⁓

A couple weeks later, in April, I was invited to fly to Chicago. One of my college roommates, Jill Malcolm, had always joked with me that if I was ever on *Oprah*, she wanted to be there. She was one of the Baltimore coordinators and did a magnificent job with her chapter. Her flight arrived at O'Hare at roughly the same time as mine. We shared the limo ride to the hotel, chatted about old times and were equally thrilled at this new turn of events for Project Linus. It was our first opportunity to spend time together since my divorce. At this juncture, I really needed time with one of my best friends. Betsy and Joni, another Headquarters volunteer, met us at the Omni Hotel. We all shared a very generous suite. I was also given meal vouchers to the hotel's restaurant. Once again, we were enjoying star treatment.

Jill and I giggled our way through dinner. Some of the people in this semi-formal restaurant appeared better attired for a biker bar. The waiter came over to apologize for these rowdy, loud and disruptive diners. He clued us in that guests for the Jerry Springer show also stayed at the Omni and were given the same vouchers as Oprah's guest. It wasn't hard to pick out the Springer guests. They were behaving in much the same fashion as the guests typically do on his shows, aside from taking off their clothes or throwing punches. I always thought those were antics planned to get a rise from the audience, but evidently it's more real than we imagine. We didn't care, though. This gave us one more unique memory to add to our mental album of this trip.

The following morning, we were all chauffeured to the Harpo studios. Joni alluded to the fact that I was in for a wonderful surprise. If I were going to the Springer studios, this would have been cause for great concern with their tabloid agenda. But being the Oprah Show, I could only imagine what great thing that meant. Once again, I found myself dreaming that we were about to receive our much-needed funding—if not directly from Oprah, perhaps from a viewer who had a kind heart and a lucrative bank account. The girls were escorted to their seats in the audience, and I was taken back to a communal green room.

At the hotel that morning, I hadn't spent much time on my hair or makeup, since experience taught me that the professionals at the show would do a great job getting me ready for the cameras. Television makeup is completely different than what we normally wear in public, so I was more than happy to heed to their skill and know-how. When I was called back into the hair and makeup chair, the stylist seemed frazzled. She looked at me and said I looked fine. *What?* I hadn't even applied mascara that morning. I'd come with a clean face in anticipation of the stylist's magic touch. After a little persuading, the makeup artist agreed to work her charm. In short order, I was camera ready. Outwardly,

I was now prepared to meet the public at large. Inwardly, alarms were beginning to sound.

The segment was called "Oprah's Angels." Oprah's producers had chosen three efforts to highlight. In addition to Project Linus, there was an inner city effort, and a husband and wife team, also from Colorado. I had the chance to get to know the couple while we all waited. They had lost a son to suicide and created a special program where high school students could give a special yellow card when they knew they were in serious mental torment. This card was known by the school teachers, counselors, fellow students and parents alike. When the student flashed the card, it was a significant signal for everyone to stop what they were doing and immediately focus on the situation. A teen was letting the authority figures know he or she was considering suicide.

We learned that one of our charities would be receiving a $45,000 award. I suggested that since we were all doing great things, we might consider splitting it evenly, no matter which of us was the lucky recipient. Fifteen thousand dollars would go a long way for Project Linus. The Colorado couple agreed wholeheartedly. The other gentleman however didn't seem at all interested in my proposition.

We were given our order of appearance, and I was slated to go last. Thanks to a lifetime of competitive sports, I am used to preparing myself mentally through imagery. I've also developed a routine before meeting with the media—I center myself and say a prayer that the right words will come out of my mouth, connecting me with the audience and opening their hearts to our cause. Mostly, though, I don't want to say something foolish that will reflect negatively on our whole organization. Some shows give a heads-up of what the questions will be, but that wasn't the case on *Oprah*. As I waited, I reflected on Project Linus stories that the audience might find interesting and inspire the viewers to action.

The Colorado couple went first, and as they were wrapping up, an assistant came rushing in and said I was on next. I told her that I'd been told I'd be going on last, but she said that I was now to be second. I asked the assistant for a moment to collect my thoughts but was told there was no time. She told me—with a strong sense of urgency—that we needed to be on stage immediately. I desperately wanted a few seconds to say a quick prayer but there was no time.

I'm used to the music world where concerts are often held in large venues that can accommodate anywhere from hundreds to tens of thousands of people. It was always surprising to see how small the audience area actually is for a television show, even though from the viewer's vantage point, it looks huge. That had been my experience when I visited the *Saturday Night Live* set and *David Letterman*. Once again, it proved true on *Oprah's* set.

There were two chairs set center stage. I entered from behind the stage and immediately zoomed in on Oprah seated in the left-hand chair facing the audience. I was so excited to finally meet her. Many an afternoon I'd laughed and cried with her through a variety of guests and topics. She's always exuded the feeling that she is everyone's girlfriend. Now, she and I were finally going to be face to face. I truly felt the anticipation of reuniting with a long-lost friend.

As I approached, Oprah stood and gave me a quick handshake. She motioned for me to have a seat. She gave me a smile and then seemed to mentally go somewhere else, preoccupied in her own thoughts. Complete silence enveloped us. The moment was surreal. Here I was, sitting in a chair opposite Oprah. Everything I'd dreamed of for Project Linus was coming to fruition. The years of devotion, dedication, hard work, and selfless giving to children in need by everyone involved with Project Linus were about to be rewarded. My heart swelled with joy and gratitude for this opportunity.

The audience was merrily chatting amongst themselves. On stage, however, you could have heard a pin drop. There was none of the casual chitchat or ice breaking that I'd previously experienced before the cameras start to roll. Just complete silence. My heart began to deflate, and I felt a sinking sensation in the pit of my stomach. Finally, after what seemed like an eternity (in reality it was probably only 15 seconds) I decided to try to warm up Oprah.

"Oprah, do you see that lady in the audience?" I asked as I pointed out Jill. "She and I used to be roommates at the University of Maryland, and we watched you every morning before classes, when you were on the Baltimore morning show, *People are Talking*. Oprah seemed completely disinterested and simply responded with, "Baltimore. Baltimore, Baltimore, Baltimore." Evidently her memories of Baltimore aren't very happy ones and I'd chosen a topic that was neither near nor dear, to her. But at the time, I had no idea of her history there. I felt that I'd been shut down. The sinking feeling grew stronger.

We sat in silence until the director gave the signal that we were about to begin. At that moment, it was as if someone turned on a switch in Oprah. Her body came to life, her eyes sparkled and she made a quick joke to the audience. Everyone was happy except me. I was thoroughly confused. What was going on? I had no idea how to respond to this energy shift.

The segment didn't in actuality end up being about Project Linus—not much anyway. It was focused on me, which made me quite uncomfortable. After all, I'd come here with the hope and anticipation of propelling Project Linus forward to new levels of growth—not to focus on my journey with Project Linus. When Oprah asked the classic questions about how I was inspired to start the effort, I became a little more at ease. This was very familiar territory. As Joni predicted, a wonderful surprise occurred when they showed a video with Laura Williams, the little girl I originally saw in the *Parade* magazine article. For years, we lovingly referred to her as the beautiful face that launched hundreds of blankets, which grew to thousands and eventually millions! She was our poster child—frozen in our minds as that one image of the three-year-old cancer patient.

Apparently, the Harpo staff located her in California. She was now eight years old with a full head of hair. She looked very much like the healthy, active girl she was. It was such a treat to see this sweet child growing into a beautiful young lady. In hindsight, I wish I had asked for a copy of Laura's address to reconnect with her. My mind raced ahead, and I was sure they were going to bring Laura out on stage. "After five years," I thought, "they are about to provide me the opportunity to meet my inspiration." My heart beat with eager expectancy.

Instead of Laura, two adorable young girls paraded across the stage with a large rectangular object in their hands. "OK," I thought, "it's not Laura, but it's something we really need for our organization." As the girls came closer, my mind screamed, "It's one of those jumbo checks! Finally our prayers are being answered. Money—a huge amount, actually—oh, all the things we'll be able to do with that $45,000!" What a vivid imagination I seem to have.

Rather than a large rectangular representation of money, I was presented with a gorgeous quilt with the words "Thank you Karen" sewn into it—a quilt that had been painstakingly created by one of our own coordinators, Carol Babbitt. The segment then quickly drew to a close. I was numb and in a bit of shock. It felt as if I was being summarily dismissed as I was led to a seat in the audience near my friends. That previous sinking feeling became a hollow sensation in the pit my stomach, and I felt tears sting my eyes.

Nothing had gone as I'd imagined. I sat there, as if in a trance, trying to make sense of what just happened. Remember the scene from *A Christmas Story* when the little boy, Ralphie, has waited with great anticipation to meet Santa so he can tell him he wants a Red Ryder BB gun and then he freezes up when the big moment arrives? That was exactly how I was feeling. I couldn't help thinking that I'd forgotten to say something important—something that would have made Oprah understand how much Project Linus needed this infusion of aid. Jill, Betsy and Joni were very congratulatory and said sweet, encouraging things to me, but no one knew the depths of despair I was experiencing at that very moment.

From the audience, we witnessed the final segment of the day. I watched dumbfounded as the last guest not only received a brand new minivan to use for his charity, but the monetary prize as well. He was doing wonderful things, and I was very happy for him, but I couldn't help feeling as if I'd been given the booby-prize.

My thoughts drifted to Carol—the coordinator and quilter

extraordinaire—knowing she was as frazzled as the rest of us. Carol was a super busy mom as well as a Project Linus coordinator with a booming chapter. The last thing I wanted to do was tax my own people. Obviously, she had been pressed by the Harpo staff to make the quilt. In the grand scheme of things, I'm sure she was thrilled to be asked to take on this project for Oprah, but it just seemed like one more kick in the Project Linus gut. *A blanket? Really???* It was absolutely stunning and in my favorite colors of blues and greens. But, to be honest, the last thing I needed at that time was one more blanket. My house was teeming with blankets. A blanket wasn't going to pay our bills. Nor was it going to help us hire a much-needed staff member.

After the show, we were given Oprah "Thank You" coffee mugs. We were then taken for a tour of the studio and had the opportunity to spend time with the Chicago coordinators. I went through these happenings in a daze. Fortunately, I remembered that I had hand-carried a Linus "get well soon" card for Oprah to sign and gave it to one of her assistants. The first response was, "Oprah doesn't give autographs." I actually wasn't asking for an autograph. This was a special card for a sweet boy who was one of my friend's children. He had cerebral palsy and had just endured a horrific operation where they'd cut many of his leg tendons. He would have to spend months in a body cast lying prone on a hospital bed in their living room, hoping that some day he would be able to walk. I didn't want her autograph—I wanted Oprah to give him and his family a little boost to get through this difficult time. I pushed the card back into her hand and asked her to please try.

I felt relieved to have the show over, but wondered if it

had seemed as awkward to the viewers as it did to me. My dear friend and fellow Toastmaster, Elissa, once explained that there are always three speeches—the one you plan to give, the one you give and the one you wish you gave. On our drive back to the airport, Jill assured me that many people were going to be inspired by the segment and great things were in store for Project Linus. I hoped she was right.

As I sat on the plane heading back to Denver, the skies were clear but dark clouds returned to my thoughts. It felt as if my big pie-in-the-sky dream of saving Project Linus had just been squashed. That aspiration now seemed lost forever—vanished into thin air like the vapors of our plane's contrail. Instead of a generous check, I was returning home with a blanket. I felt like I'd let the whole organization down, and the reverie of being saved by Oprah's show felt as stale as yesterday's news.

CHAPTER
22

If You Love Somebody, Set Them Free

If you don't like something, change it.
If you can't change it, change your attitude.

\- Maya Angelou

Everyone wants to know what it is like to meet Oprah. The best and most accurate word I can come up with is "unforgettable." The last thing I want to do is "diss" the person who gave us an amazing opportunity, but I also don't want to sugarcoat the experience. Someone rightly pointed out that my experience was probably comparable that of most non-celebrity guests. This insight was confirmed by one of my friends who'd also been a guest on *Oprah*. She too had a similar "adventure." What a revelation!

Being a guest on the *Oprah* show has become the platinum standard for success in our modern society. It certainly provides an instantaneous gold star for one's resume and a door opener to future opportunities—somewhat like winning an Academy Award or Olympic gold medal. In hindsight, I appreciate that the occasion to be on her show was a true gift. Early on however I wasn't feeling so grateful. It took time to work through my feelings and expectations of the "Oprah" experience.

That Oprah didn't welcome me with the open armed embrace of a long lost girlfriend was certainly not her fault. I felt like we had history because I'd seen her so often in the media. But for her, I was a complete stranger. It was completely unrealistic for me to expect her to treat me with the same kind of familiarity she gives her celebrity guests. I'd witnessed this uneasiness on countless occasions between Ginger and his fans. I should have known better. I had expected Oprah to treat every guest in the welcoming and amiable manner that comes through the television screen— whether the cameras are rolling or not.

Expecting that Project Linus might receive the $45,000 award was again an unwarranted hope. By now, that prize money would have been long gone, yet the exposure Oprah afforded us has been priceless. Oprah offered a platform that enabled Project Linus to reach millions of viewers. I subsequently discovered that Oprah signed the get-well card I'd left with her assistant and it was joyously received by him and his family. My friends were grateful for the uplifting encouragement her sentiments represented—another priceless outcome. The positive ripple effects from that show continue to this day.

Since the show wasn't seen on the same day as it was taped,

we went into post-national publicity mode and optimistically positioned ourselves for the onslaught of interest that would be received once the show aired. Unfortunately, there were a few glitches that occurred, which may have decreased the initial interest we received. During my segment, the name Project Linus was hardly spoken, so viewers had to listen closely to catch the name of our effort. Also, when people went to Oprah's website to learn more about our organization, the list of charities appeared in alphabetical order, beginning with ABC Quilts. Guess where many of our potential Blanketeers were diverted?

Yet, miraculously, thousands of new Blanketeers still found us, and we continued to grow—more and more chapters; more and more blankets; more and more letters; more and more emails; more and more phone calls. *More and more of everything, except the one thing we needed most of all—money.* There continued to be less and less funds to support Project Linus. Not only did we now have new added expenses, we had also lost our main benefactor, Ginger, to his life in South Africa. Although he continued to be a fan of our work, the open checkbook was now half-a-world away and permanently closed to Project Linus.

In June, we held our Second Annual Conference in Denver. It was so uplifting to meet face to face with our coordinators. It also served as a wonderful diversion and opportunity for me to look at our circumstances through a different lens—hope. I loved the coordinators' enthusiasm, energy and belief that Project Linus was a cause worthy of their time and talents.

"Show and Tell" continued to be one of my favorite parts of

the conference. Once again, coordinators shared unforgettable stories about their chapters. They proudly imparted tales about special Blanketeers, memorable deliveries and noteworthy anecdotes depicting the uniqueness of their chapters. Although we communicated numbers of blankets delivered, "Show and Tell" was never a competition. Some people had just started their chapter, others had been up and running for years. Some people lived in rural areas and others in the big city. Some coordinators were gregarious, while others were painfully shy. Some were affiliated with a church, scout troop or a community organization that was assisting them, whereas others were flying solo. Some people were in their own personal battle with illness. Others had just lost a spouse or loved one. We were all in different stages of life and embraced one another for what we were doing.

We were all equals at conference—an instantly warm and welcoming family. If one person had a dilemma, there were dozens of ideas offered to solve it. No longer did we have to bear our problems on our own. We had a whole army, the Project Linus family, backing us up. National conference really drove that point home.

We had an extraordinary treat that year. Debbie Mumm, the renowned quilt and fabric designer, as well as distinctive artist of oh-so-many-cute home items, generously flew to Colorado to be our special guest. Debbie was an early fan of our work, and our appreciation of her talents was reciprocal. I even had her autograph some of her charming signature ironing board covers for my mom and Tina (who has always been a huge ironing fan). Having Debbie with us at national conference really was a feather in our caps.

Betsy and the Headquarters staff did a wonderful job

making sure all the nuts and bolts were taken care of—handouts, snacks and the essentials for a three-day conference. Betsy's three daughters didn't fall far from the tree. They had been taught through example at an early age the importance of helping others. Mindy, Nicky and Christina immediately had a couple dozen new aunts and a few uncles, too!

> *"I still can remember the picture of the little girl in the newspaper article that first interested my mother in Project Linus. I remember the excitement Mom felt in becoming a part of something that was so meaningful to others. When she first got started, I helped to make a blanket here and there, but she always did most of the work.*
>
> *"As I entered high school, and was required to do community service, my first thought was Project Linus. I remember organizing emails, chapter information, mailing letters, helping with conferences and all that entailed, as well as helping to run the behind the scenes show. Although it has been many years since I was a huge part of helping, I do remember spending many hours with my mother doing so much more than making blankets.*
>
> *"For years, I don't think I actually made a blanket of my own, and I don't believe my mother made many either. This is all because she was dedicated to organizing all the contact information and keeping the program growing and growing. I remember having several meetings at the kitchen table in our house, with all the ladies working out conference information, "Make a Blanket Days," and*

discussing how to get others involved. I even remember when Project Linus made it to the Oprah show.

"In my opinion, I think my mother always loved that I could help with the organizational part of Project Linus. As an organized person myself, I recall helping to file important contact information, talking with people on the phone so they could get in contact with coordinators, and taking care of many mailings to get the word out. As well, when blankets came in, I remember sorting through them and getting them ready for delivery to hospitals.

"Just a year or two ago, my husband and I participated in a blanket-making day, and I had a wonderful time organizing the many blankets people made into piles to go to a variety of different places that needed them for kids. I have to say that although Project Linus is all about the blankets, I always enjoyed doing all the other things that got those wonderful blankets into kids' arms.

"I'm not much of a quilter, but I sure can organize and be a leader. That is what I always enjoyed about Project Linus. There was something for everyone to help with. Not to forget, I remember a time when I helped my mother contact a group I believe was "Project Open Heart" which took blankets to an orphanage overseas. I recall the stories that were told about how the orphans were so thrilled to have a blanket to call their own.

"Although I was never part of making the blankets,

I feel like all that other "stuff" was just as important. And for years, my mother was a huge part of making that all happen. Now, we spend "Black Friday" shopping for endless amounts of flannel fabric, so my mom can sew her heart out all year long and continue to make a difference in kids' lives. Every single time she sits down at her sewing machine, she makes it work until the needle just can't go up and down any more. I still have hanging in my classroom a tiny little promotional blanket that the Project Linus gals made—with the cute Project Linus label—and I tell all of my students about how they can make a difference in this world, in one way or another, just like my mother taught me.

"Man, was she dedicated to Project Linus, as if she was making billions of dollars. Here she is today, still working that hard to give back. I must say, although my mother may have been stressed from time to time trying to keep up with everyone's needs as they created more and more Project Linus chapters, she sure taught me and my sisters a very valuable lesson: make a difference and give back to the world any way that you can.

"Project Linus gave my mom a great start after moving to Colorado and leaving many friends behind in Texas. A great start for her, for her daughters, for people who wanted to give back, and for all those children that have ever received a Project Linus blanket. Thank you Project Linus for letting me be

> *a part of the growth and outreach that continues to*
> *makes you such a thriving organization today. It was*
> *great fun to be a part of those very first years of when*
> *one person started a great project that then allowed*
> *me and my mother to connect in a very special way,*
> *bringing us together and giving hope and joy, one*
> *child at a time."*
>
> *Mindy Elliott Turner*

After the conference, everything about Project Linus seemed to go numb for me. While in the middle of turmoil, it is hard to get one's bearings. I was going through many pressure-laden events. There was the shock and awe of divorce, followed by the Oprah experience, followed by putting on a national conference. In addition, there was the daily onslaught of Project Linus, leaving an overwhelming, enormous, cherry-on-top, sundae of stress. Although most of our coordinators were extremely self-sufficient and an absolute joy to work with, I couldn't help empathizing with Old Mother Hubbard. It felt like our cupboards were bare and unruly children wouldn't stop tugging at my skirt for attention or fighting amongst themselves.

The increase of strain was creating tension within the Headquarters team. As much as I loved Project Linus, I needed to find a full-time job to support myself. Unlike my other Headquarters co-workers, I no longer had a husband to support me. Financial responsibility lay squarely on my shoulders—something had to give. Since I couldn't support myself with this volunteer venture, Project Linus was becoming less and less of a priority for me. Sure, I was still delivering blankets, still giving talks, and publicity was still being generated, but my heart was in it less and less. I was in survival mode and felt alone and on my own.

Betsy was our rock during this entire storm. She kept working to keep things anchored. Eventually, it became even too much for her excellent skills—it felt as if Project Linus, along with our entire team, was adrift in a sea of chaos and despair. Maybe the best thing to do was just let it sink.

That fall, Betsy sent out a letter to all of the coordinators letting them know that Project Linus was going to close our doors on December 31, 2000, five years after we started. We had succeeded in making a difference in the lives of hundreds of thousands of children and their families, so we would end on a high note.

I have since learned that five years is often the magical turning point for many businesses. Successful ones have to decide if they are going to stay small and comfortable or stretch their wings and evolve to the next level. Struggling businesses have to decide whether to continue with their efforts or close their doors. Both sets of answers can be correct choices, depending on what business owners want and what future prospects look like from their vantage points.

As for Project Linus, we were exhausted—mentally and physically worn out. Our tanks were on empty. Betsy encouraged the coordinators to continue making blankets and delivering them to their recipients, just not under the auspices of Project Linus. After all, we hadn't invented the security blanket, just a way of banding together groups of people with a shared desire to help children.

You can imagine the shock and dismay many of the

coordinators had in response to this news. I'm sure it came from left field for most of them. They had no idea the amount of pressure or the workload we had endured because we never complained about any of it beyond our small inner circle. We heard a wide gambit of responses from quite a few people. Some quietly and dutifully closed their chapters and returned to their normal lives. Others expressed anger that we were not able to keep things going. Still others peeled off and tried to make their own Project Linus, name included!

The best response came with a call came from Bloomington, Illinois. It was our Utah coordinator and Oprah quilt maker extraordinaire, Carol Babbitt, who had recently moved to Illinois. After receiving the "we're closing" letter, Carol and Mary Balagna, a Forsyth, Illinois coordinator, got together and wondered if Project Linus could be saved.

> *"Mary and I met at the 2nd annual conference and we were immediate friends. I had no idea just how close we would become over the next few months. (After receiving the closing letter) I felt so strongly that Project Linus needed to continue, that we had so much more that we could accomplish, and that we were really only in our infancy. I was really compelled to do this. I knew that in order to be successful, I would need the help and support of my husband and my two boys. Thankfully they were 100% on board and always have been. I couldn't do this without them. And I was so lucky to meet Mary when I did. I really feel that it was meant to be. She agreed to*

> *come on board as the Vice President and my business partner, and it has been an arrangement truly made in heaven. Over the years we have worked side by side with our husbands and families and it has been the highlight of my life."*
>
> *Carol Babbitt*

Carol and Mary performed their due diligence and spent time interviewing Betsy and me—learning about what had gone right as well as those elements that had gone wrong. With this knowledge, much prayer and discussions with their husbands, Kirk and Terry, they proposed to take over the administration of Project Linus on October 30, 2000. Wisely, however, they wouldn't take it in its current state. There were some aspects of our operation that needed to be started anew. Most of what needed to be fixed with Project Linus came as a result of us not having a clear growth plan from the get-go, when we were first picking up steam. We had simply learned to put out fires along the way.

The organization had not been started with the vision of becoming what it was in the year 2000. I never really understood way back in the beginning of this adventure that many of the actions I took to simply get more blankets for more children would become the fertilizer for growth beyond my wildest dreams. Initially, I'd intended Project Linus to be a little grassroots effort—an effort that miraculously received a super dose of Miracle Grow because of the outpouring of love from around the world.

Carol asked me what I wanted my role to be with the new

organization, and I replied that I wanted to be a coordinator. I wanted to get back to the fun stuff—making blankets, inspiring other Blanketeers and making deliveries. That's what I enjoyed. Yet, these were the pieces I'd had to put on the back burner because of all the other administrative duties that needed attention. Like a fairy godmother, Carol waved her magic wand and poof—it was done!

The new Headquarters created a contract which each and every coordinator had to sign. It stated the basic rules of the organization. Despite the blood, sweat and tears that went into the changeover of administrations, from the outside, most people didn't even notice much of a change at all. The transition worked rather seamlessly.

CHAPTER
23

Brand New Day

I can't moan about any of it.
I had a great time in the goldfish bowl.

\- Robert Plant

With the advent of the New Year 2001, all things felt possible once again. It was as if the world had been lifted off my shoulders. Knowing that Project Linus was off to a bright restart and in very capable hands felt like a phoenix rising from the ashes. No longer did I have to focus on the day-to-day machinations required to run a national charity. It was time to get back to the basics and enjoy my favorite parts of Project Linus—making blankets, motivating others to make a difference, coordinating blanket-making events, collecting the finished products and delivering to the extraordinary young recipients.

I was again able to stroll down the yarn aisle at the local

craft shop and brainstorm color combos that might bring joy to a child—an activity I'd rarely had time to do over the past few years. Shimmering aqua with a bright lime green or puckering lemon-yellow with juicy tangerine orange, or a patriotic red, white and blue—the combos were limitless, and the thrill of planning out the next blanket was as fun as holding the finished product. Over these past few years, it seemed the only time I'd been able to crochet was while taking fire academy and emergency medical technician classes or while on a cramped airplane—not exactly relaxing circumstances, to say the least.

The change from being the Project Linus "everything-person" to becoming the Denver area coordinator left me with a comfortable and manageable workload. Once again, I was able to enjoy setting up speaking engagements and motivating people in my own community. I no longer cringed when we received local or national publicity, knowing that the extra workload required on a coordinator level would be completely manageable. Instead of racing in to drop off bags of blankets at delivery sites, I was able to stop in and meet the patients as well as meet with hospital staff and learn how we could best serve their needs. Project Linus was pleasurable once again!

Early that year, I was presented with a wonderful honor, the TOYA award—Ten Outstanding Young Americans— by the Jaycees. The Jaycees are The United States Junior Chamber of Commerce, and they give people between the ages of 18 and 40 the tools they need to build the bridges of success for themselves. They focus on the areas of business development, management skills, individual training, community service and international connections. The annual award is bestowed upon recipients the organization believes to be "the best, brightest and most inspirational leaders America has to offer."

The Jaycees started to add women to the mix of recipients in 1986. Of the more than 600 individuals who have received this honor, such notable recipients include Presidents John F. Kennedy, Richard Nixon, Gerald Ford and Bill Clinton, and Vice Presidents Al Gore and Richard Cheney. Also honored were Howard Hughes, Orson Wells, Elvis Presley, Nelson Rockefeller, dogsled champion Susan Butcher, Jesse Jackson and Christopher Reeves. As an alumni recipient, my name appears directly above boxer extraordinaire Joe Louis! I was flown to Washington, D.C. and found myself amidst quite impressive company. They included:

- Mark Hamilton Eckhardt—founder of an organization to grant college scholarships to musically talented inner city youth
- Heather French Henry—former Miss America who serves as an advocate for homeless veterans
- Suzanne Greenberg—Executive Director/President of the Child Abuse and Neglect Council
- Robin Lorraine Hartl—co-host of *HomeTime* and a spokesperson for Habitat for Humanity
- Cathy Robinson—a career HIV and AIDS educator and advocate
- Army Lt. Col. George Peoples Jr., MD—a world-class, trained surgeon working on preventative vaccines targeting the majority of cancers
- Air Force Major Timothy James Lawrence—excelling

in the field of space research
- Richard Leonard Tafel—founder of the Log Cabin Republicans, the nation's largest gay and lesbian Republican organization
- Michele Tafoya—sports commentator and a member of the Board of Directors for The American Refugee Committee, which provides humanitarian assistance and training to refugees and displaced persons seeking to enable them to rebuild productive lives of dignity and purpose
- Da Vinci's Notebook—an a cappella quartet

Not only was it exciting to get all dolled up and receive acknowledgement for all the hard work that had been accomplished over the past five years, but it was also nice to have my family present for this event, since it took place in my hometown area.

~⟞

Melanie, one of my workout partners and friends from church, found a job for me at her husband's company, Bailey's Allied Van Lines. They needed someone to help with coordinating commercial office moves, and it was something I could do from the comforts of my new home. During the spring I had sold the ranch and moved closer in to the town of Parker on a quiet, suburban cul-de-sac. My new home came with a gorgeous view of the Front Range, and I was surrounded with young families and friendly neighbors.

That summer, I was also able to pursue other interests in my life. My motorcycle-riding skills were honed with trips through the scenic Rocky Mountains and into neighboring states. I was able to visit my high school friend—and a Los

Angeles coordinator—Brenda, who was also a Los Angeles coordinator, while she stayed in Amsterdam. I adopted a six-year-old border collie from the local shelter, Denver Dumb Friends League, who became my constant companion. I took up rowing at the Cherry Creek Reservoir. Additionally, it was time for my 20-year Wakefield High School reunion, and I found it incredibly uplifting to catch up with friends who had dropped off my radar. Remember, this was pre-Facebook, so keeping up with friends was a much more tedious task than now. Thank you, Mark Zuckerberg!

As a single woman living by myself, I decided that taking a taekwondo class would be a good idea for a few different reasons. I wanted to develop skills, should I need to defend myself—even if it just meant removing *me* from a situation (although a good axe kick to the shoulder wouldn't be a bad tool to master either). Martial arts is a fabulous form of exercise—mentally and physically—and a magnificent discipline-builder.

I met some wonderful people at Parker Academy of Martial Arts—including our hilarious and animated instructors, Fred and Rob. A hulking Australian bloke named Warren kept us amused and was quite a deft martial artist. Sherry was such an inspirational classmate. Her book *Broken but Not Forsaken* not only shares her incredible story of surviving cancer, widowhood and a fatal train accident, but she also shares her speaking skills by educating the public about the hazards of train crossings. She was the individual who had also appeared on *Oprah*.

Then there was Gary. He ended up being everything I had written about on my wish list for a future life partner—fiscally responsible, fun, active, enjoyed travel, had a strong sense of family, and an added bonus—he didn't mind that I rode motorcycles. In fact, he had a BMW of his own. At the time, I had a BMW and a Harley, so we were able to enjoy breathtaking rides up the sweeping mountain passes and take in some of the other scenic opportunities the Rocky Mountains had to offer.

⁓

By the time my parents came out for their annual visit in the fall, Gary and I were in a budding romance. We had become regulars in an early-morning kickboxing class at the gym taught by our taekwondo instructor Fred. After a morning class, I noticed one of our workout partners racing out of the gym. We chided her for skipping her normal weight-lifting routine, and she replied, "Our country is being attacked. I have to leave now." I know she used to work for one of the secret-service-type agencies. I never saw her again. We raced upstairs to where the gym televisions were and witnessed a moment the world will never forget—the live view of the second plane crashing into the Twin Towers.

I had given my parents my room during their visit since it contained a king-sized bed and a television. They were both awake when I returned home around 8 a.m. Feelings of déjà vu sparked my memories as I crawled between them on the bed, just like I did so many other mornings during childhood, decades earlier. We watched dumbfounded as the second twin tower melted like a standing stick of butter in a microwave. *Holy cow! What was happening?* Everyone was speculating, and news came in reporting the Pentagon and Pennsylvania crashes. My parents still lived in the home I grew up in, just a few miles from the Pentagon.

Being an adult, it was interesting to observe my parents as they experienced this world tragedy. I saw two different sides of my own personality expressed through each of them. My mother was excited to get home to see if any damage had been done to our house and talk with our neighbors about this event. My father, on the other hand, was adamant they weren't going anywhere. At that time, we had no idea who was responsible for this atrocity and how far-reaching their plans might be. Ultimately, it didn't matter if my dad had agreed to head right home, because all the airports were immediately closed. Flights wouldn't resume for days.

As time went on, some questions were answered, others were not. I'll never forget the eerie silence of the skies. The rare exception seemed to be at night. I lay in the guest room listening to the fighter planes patrolling the Denver air space. It gave me a tiny glimpse of what it must have been like to live in Europe during the world wars. No, we didn't have air raids or bombs dropping on us, but it was still a very unsettling time. My folks kept themselves glued to the television for the latest breaking news. I stayed as far away from the set as possible—I have little tolerance for speculative journalism. Under silent skies, my dad and I planted a row of arbor vitae on the north side of my home, providing an excuse to get outside and away from the constant conjecture of the media. The computer and my crochet hook became fully employed. It helped to reach out to friends around the country during this unsettling time.

Project Linus again became a source of great comfort. During a time when everyone else was paralyzed with grief and bewilderment, the Project Linus army found itself empowered and immediately started pulling resources together to assist the victims' families in New York and Washington, D.C. We understood how to help when tragedy struck, and we knew how to pool our efforts to make a big difference for many.

Two things stick out in Betsy Elliott's mind from this event. The first was the readiness of Project Linus to help. After we all got over the initial shock of what had taken place, we went into Project Linus-mode and began contacting each other. JoAnn Holley, our Northern Virginia coordinator, handled blankets for the Pentagon. Another coordinator in New York had a contact at the main hospital in New York, St. Vincent's. Every coordinator who could was ready, willing and able to send blankets. It was just a matter of finding the proper channels for distribution of these items to the victims' children, grandchildren, nieces and nephews.

The second event that made a strong impression on Betsy was the lack of survivors. She remembers that there was no one to give blankets to at the local hospitals. She recalls that the emergency room doctors and nurses were just standing around waiting for the injured to come in, and initially there weren't any. Project Linus had to wait until things settled down. Afterward, we worked with the fallen firefighter and police chaplains to get blankets to the children of those who had died.

JoAnn is the same coordinator who was on the *Rosie O'Donnell Show*. She heard that there was a temporary command center set up for Pentagon victims' families at the Crystal City Sheraton. Two days after the horrifying events occurred, she loaded up her car and at 4:30 in the morning, made the 32-mile roundtrip drive to the Pentagon area. Her plan was to drop the blankets at the front desk of the hotel before the big commute started and still be able to get to work on time.

When she arrived at the front desk, JoAnn was instructed to go upstairs to the ballroom where efforts were being coordinated. She recalls being shaky with nervousness when a kind uniformed gentleman approached her and tried to help calm her down. JoAnn assumed he was a chaplain, because he was so composed and soft-spoken. She felt like a "dithering idiot" as she blurted out her reason for being there. Quickly, the gentleman asked soldiers to go with JoAnn and help haul up the many blankets. She left her contact information in case she could be of further assistance.

By late afternoon, JoAnn received a call. It was from someone who was calling on behalf of the man she'd met that morning, "General So-and-so!" She had no idea he was a general. In fact, she "wouldn't have known the difference between a general and a corporal." When I asked her if she had noticed any stars on his uniform, she giggled that she was definitely seeing stars but they were more from her nervousness rather than the identification of military rank!

The general wanted to thank JoAnn as well as invite her to bring more blankets. On her second drive home from the Pentagon area, she was so energized with how Project Linus was able to make a difference that she called a local radio station. She excitedly blurted out to the screener the many opportunities available to those looking for avenues to assist victims' families beyond simply writing a check. One of the tangible ways—they could make a blanket! The screener immediately had JoAnn speak live on the radio, and by the time she returned home, there were already almost a dozen messages from potential Blanketeers awaiting instructions on how to proceed. Knitters, quilters, crocheters—they all wanted to help.

JoAnn was invited to return to the Sheraton the following week for an update and to bring more blankets. She brought her son Spencer with her so he could experience "what Mom does and why she does it." She also invited Washington, D.C. coordinator, Connie Totten-Oldham, to participate. JoAnn remembers being heartbroken as she listened to mothers with children in tow inquiring if their husbands had been located. Then, horrification set in as she heard the General explain that their loved ones might never be found because of the explosive destruction caused by the impact. They might be lucky to retrieve a wedding band, if that had even survived.

Ultimately, through teamwork, we were able to deliver over 10,000 Project Linus blankets to New York City and over 600 to the Pentagon families of the deceased. Like Columbine, we were all dealing with new territory and a whole new situation. But we knew we could make a difference, and we did.

CHAPTER
24

The Men... Exposed!

No man stands so tall as when he stoops to help a child.

- Abraham Lincoln

When we started our national conferences, I was able to meet coordinators' husbands and witness the partnerships that occurred between the couples. Project Linus is, by and large, coordinated by women. But when I speak with coordinators, a resounding theme emerges. They couldn't be the effective coordinators they are without the help of their families.

My ex-husband Ginger gets credit for funding the organization during its early years. We could not have grown to the scale we did in such a quick fashion without having received his financial backing. He was my early sounding board and never complained about all the chaos of blankets and volunteers that filled our home.

Betsy's husband Mark was also a great sport throughout the early years of Project Linus. As we grew and developed a Board, the Elliott house was often our central meeting location. For years, their house was a drop-off site, which meant their home and garage served as a temporary storage space for many-a-blanket. Mark gave up his home office to Betsy so she could have a defined space for all of her work. He was also very accommodating when it came to last-minute dinner plans because Betsy experienced a busy or frustrating day.

Sandy and Lew Wyatt are adorable. They are from Reidsville, North Carolina and radiate Southern charm. Sandy first learned about Project Linus from a *Family Circle* article. She was an avid knitter. We seemed like a great match for her passion. Lew was retired by then, and the two worked together as a dynamic duo, with her as a coordinator and him as "the trucking company and lugger."

Lew is one of those fun guys who—within minutes after meeting him—you swear you've known him all your life. During conferences, he was often the ringleader. He was able to rally fellow husbands (including my Dad) to go on side trips to the Caterpillar plant, ball games and the shooting range. He encouraged the addition of testosterone to the crafting classes and even participated in the men's quilt challenge. One year, we had a purse-making class, and his ended up being one of the cutest ones created. He made it for his granddaughter, of course!

During a weak moment at conference one year, he admitted giving up his hobby room to Sandy's Project Linus efforts. Sandy observed that his so-called "weak moment" benefitted him as well—he now has a two-story barn that includes television, air-conditioning, heat and a telephone to support his hobbies. With all the work required from a coordinator, Sandy and Lew agreed that you don't think about Project Linus—you just do it.

Judy Bell of Fort Worth found Project Linus through the *Parade* magazine article. Even though she was working at the time, she was still able to cultivate a thriving chapter. Judy drove out to the first conference with her husband Jess, and they were impressed by the general warmth and enthusiasm shown by everyone. Soon, we were calling Jess by his nickname "Sweet Thang," and he good-naturedly put up with our chiding. Despite some efforts over the years to get Judy to retire as coordinator, he has relented. He doesn't want to be a "monster to the ladies." He has always been a huge help with blanket transportation, and still is.

Patty Gregory of St. Louis originally spotted a segment on Project Linus through Alex Anderson's quilting show on HGTV. Her niece died of brain cancer, and she wanted to do something to honor her. As soon as she saw the Project Linus spot, she knew that we would be a great match with her quilting passion. Her husband John has attended many conferences and is very committed to Project Linus. They even moved to a larger house so they could have a three-car garage. Patty remembers that John's only stipulation was that he has at least one of the garage bays for his Harley.

Georgia's Judy Lawton discovered Project Linus one day while flipping through a *Reader's Digest*. During a conference field trip to a quilt shop, Judy's husband Frank pointed out different fabrics and remarked how certain ones would look good together. I turned to him and said, "Those are some great ideas—why don't you make a quilt, Frank?" Frank used to be a crocheter but had never tried a quilt. I was in the same boat, so he counter-challenged me. With that, the "Men's Quilt Challenge" was set. The following year, the men returned with quilts they had made. I was the sole female exception. I have to admit, mine was probably the least impressive of the bunch. The guys really took their quilting seriously and created some beautiful designs and patterns that weren't "girly" at all.

While Frank's daughter was in the military at Ft. Benning, Georgia, her Major's grandson became very ill. She furnished him with a Project Linus blanket, and the Major returned in awe. Apparently, the blanket matched his grandson's favorite colors and contained his favorite Winnie the Pooh character, Eeyore, the donkey. *How did she know?* I think a Project Linus angel told her.

Mary Sue Davis, our Dayton, Ohio coordinator, first learned about Project Linus on a *Simply Quilts* episode. She calls her husband Roy her "pack-horse." He does her pickups and drop-offs. I have always had a soft spot in my heart for Roy, because he is a swim coach and has a real passion for kids. He loves all the little things about Project Linus and once said, "If I'm having a rough day, when I deliver blankets, my cares all go away. The feeling I get when helping these children will carry me though to the end." He and Mary Sue often drive the scenic route to Bloomington, Illinois for conference in order to visit the good quilt shops along the way.

Callie, the daughter of Mobile, Alabama's coordinator, Pam Pully, had cystic fibrosis. They spent 15 years in and out of the hospital before she passed away. Each time she went to the hospital, Callie's grandmother's quilt went with her. Pam knows firsthand how near and dear the blankets are. There is an ink spot on the quilt left by a nurse who accidently laid down her pen on the blanket. Pam says that she wouldn't pay a million dollars to have that stain removed.

Pam's husband Steve is also very involved in the chapter and has melded our blankets with another charity that he is passionate about—Catch a Dream. They provide hunting and fishing trips for children in a manner similar to the Make a Wish program. He became a guide for these trips and took a Georgia boy deep-sea fishing in the Keys, where the child caught a sailfish. Another time, he took a 12-year-old girl with cancer hunting. She successfully hunted a deer and a hog in North Carolina. Steve cuts fleece for camouflage blankets that are given to seriously-ill children who are granted wishes through the Catch a Dream organization.

Janet Jarosh's husband retired from his job a few years ago. He regularly attends conferences now, makes blanket pickups and goes on "JoAnn runs."

Glen Rodgers has been a huge help to his wife Bitsey with her chapter. He makes a majority of their deliveries. Bitsey recalled an especially memorable occasion, though, when she herself did the delivery. One day, because she was "on a mission," Bitsey transformed her pickup truck into a boat. During a flashflood, she found her truck in waist-deep water, and since Bitsey only needed to travel two blocks to get to her destination, she kept her focus on transporting those blankets, no matter what. After all, she thought, the children were expecting her arrival. The blankets did make it safely; however, the truck itself was totaled.

Glen was also responsible for getting their chapter

involved with a facility called Kid's Corner, a daycare for homeless children. The facility expended their entire budget on sheets and towels used for coverings. They desperately needed blankets, and Glen recognized that Project Linus could help. The facility works with over 90 children under the age of six. When Project Linus volunteers arrived one day, they laid the blankets out, and the children were brought in by groups to pick their own blanket. One little boy asked for a blanket with Winnie the Pooh on it, and Bitsey had three for him to choose from. Another little girl asked for a pink blanket. I can guarantee that there were even more than three options for her.

Kirk Babbitt has the unique distinction of being the only male to attend the initial Project Linus National Conference way back in 1999 and has been a part of every one since then. He has always been such a good sport. I couldn't remember if his wife Carol said his name was Kirk or Kurt, so while making the conference program of attendees, we had him listed as "Mr. Babbitt." He was very good-natured about us jokingly calling him that over the weekend. Kirk continues to serve on our Board of Directors as the Director of Development, and works on building relationships for our corporate fundraising initiative. Kirk has been an important part of every conference since that first event.

As a member of the Board of Directors, Terry Balagna serves as the Project Linus liaison with United Media. Each year his quick wit and clever teaching segments are highlights for our national conferences. He cleverly reminds the coordinators of our responsibilities to the Linus image. The phase, "If you buy it, you can use it, but you can't reproduce it" has been indelibly etched into each of our minds.

His and his wife Mary's home has served as the location for memorable barbeques, pool parties and ice cream socials. I always find it ironic that this trauma and emergency room doctor has a trampoline in his backyard. He claims his family outvoted him on that decision.

I could write an entire book filled with wonderful "husband" stories. There are so many of them who have done so much to propel Project Linus forward and keep it buoyant. Although it's impossible for me to include every "husband" in this book, I can't leave this topic without giving credit to my own Mr. Wonderful—Gary. Since we first met, he has been a constant supporter of Project Linus. The company he works for, Appirio, has a strong sense of community. One day each year—Silver Lining Day—is dedicated and reserved for all employees to volunteer their time to a worthwhile cause. When Gary told them about Project Linus, they did some investigation and chose Project Linus as the main Midwest charity for their employees. It was fun and rewarding to view the mini blanket-day activities they documented on their Silver Lining Facebook page. Appirio has even incorporated Project Linus polar fleece tied blankets as a bonding activity during their orientation sessions for new employees. On more than one occasion some of their own employee's children have also been recipients of Project Linus blankets due to illness or trauma.

Although Gary has always been a staunch supporter of Project Linus, we made an agreement prior to our marriage in 2005 that the blankets would have a one-month maximum shelf-life in our home. Within a month, they need to be distributed to the children. Even though one month seems like an ample stretch of time, distribution can be an enormously time-consuming effort, especially when large amounts of blankets come in all at once.

Each blanket needs to be meticulously inspected for things that may be hazardous to the children. These include embellishments, like buttons or fringe or an errant quilting pin, or even a safety pin, that Blanketeers occasionally use to affix their contact information. For safety's sake, some coordinators have even purchased metal-detecting devices—like the ones that airport screeners use—to detect these items. We also continue to check for strong odors that can exacerbate the children's health conditions. Once the blanket has passed inspection, it receives our seal of approval—a Project Linus blanket tag. I have a wonderful group of volunteers from my church, as well as other groups who have been with me for years, who now assist with the quality control and label-sewing process to make the turnaround time much quicker.

Gary has attended national conferences with me and is a regular helper on Make a Blanket Day and Make a Difference Day quilting bees. He has made tied-fleece blankets, has schlepped blankets in and out of our home or to recipient facilities, and has answered phone calls as early as 6 a.m. (when my star Blanketeer, Teri Otsuki, ran out of yarn and assumed that the rest of the world was also awake). He's given up a room in our home for Project Linus administration and storage, and has always kept a positive attitude about the whole frenzied process.

We love our guys and couldn't do what we do without them!

Epilogue

Are You God's Wife?

Now, go take on the day!

- Dr. Laura Schlessinger

I am often asked the question, "What is it like to look at Project Linus and know you aren't running it anymore?" In complete honesty—WONDERFUL! When I hear friends talk about the joy of being a grandparent, I can absolutely relate. I look at Project Linus with pride, knowing that indeed, I was the one who set this force into motion and was able to find a way to inspire people into action. And, like a grandparent—during those "poopy times," I can hand the "baby" back to its parents and let them do the dirty work.

Carol and Mary have taken their mantel of responsibility as leaders of Project Linus very seriously. I know that they have had to make countless difficult decisions and navigate carefully through sticky situations. Like everything else in life, it is impossible to make everyone happy. Even simple things such as changing the blanket tag print from pink to blue or adding our website address to the label ruffled some feathers. I thought it was a brilliant move on their part to make these changes and know they continue to make decisions they feel will benefit the entire organization.

Both women love helping to spread the word about Project Linus and have successfully found a way to combine passion with purpose. One favorite avenue for this is through national quilting events. As talented quilters, they are helping to build the name and reputation of Project Linus while having fun together as friends.

Project Linus continues to receive national publicity. Sometimes, the media wants to take the narrative from the angle of the founder's story. It can be a highly effective approach to highlight an individual versus an organization. Viewers want to get to know the person behind the company. This was the case when we were featured a few years ago on *NBC Nightly News* with Bryan Williams. When it first aired, there were a few emails of disappointment that the focus had been on me and not the organization. Yet, it only took a few minutes before coordinators were excitedly writing to let us know that people in their own communities had already contacted them. Just as when JoAnn was on the *Rosie O'Donnell Show,* Fargo Coordinator Lynne Olien was showered with gifts by Al Roker on the *Today Show,* or I was appearing on *Oprah*, any positive publicity assists the entire effort.

Fundraising is a fact of life for most organizations. We are effectively working our way up the sponsorship ladder through the work being done by Headquarters. They have created a Friends of Project Linus distinction for businesses which provide monetary and/or product donations to aid Project Linus in our mission. Friends of Project Linus range from companies affiliated with blanket-making products—such as HandiQuilter, Quiltmaker and bernatcares.com—to mega-powers like Walmart, Exxon, Starbucks, and even a local Corvette Club. Everyone can be a Friend of Project Linus!

Last year, in 2010, we were the recipient of a generous $50,000 gift from JoAnn Fabric and Craft Stores. Immediately, there were some coordinators with their hands out expecting to receive a portion of the monies for their chapters. They weren't able to see the big picture. The chapter count at the time stood at 371. Divided equally, that would have given each chapter $134.77—not much money to make a difference. Yet, invested on a national level, Headquarters was able to hire extra office help and do things that could benefit the entire organization.

Our national conferences are now called Institutes, and they are held every other year. This is due to the amount of work that goes into putting one of these remarkable events together. It also gives coordinators a chance to save their pennies to attend—obviously, airfare, hotels and conference fees add up quickly. Perhaps, somewhere in the near future, event sponsorships will appear so that everyone who wants to attend will be able to do so.

Each year, a fun theme is selected and creatively woven throughout the Institute. The theme for summer 2011 is "It's Raining Cats and Dogs." As an animal lover, I am very excited to see what is cleverly planned. Dozens of vendors attend to impart cutting-edge techniques and donate time and products to the participants. No one goes hungry at these events either—we are showered with delicious food and snacks throughout our time together. We have more traditions which developed over the years, including Bitsey Rogers reading humorous girly stories, an annual quilt challenge, and I customarily craft a crocheted blanket during Institute to give to one of our newest coordinators. The best part is getting to be with our Project Linus family again. I think even if we held this event in a parking lot with folding chairs, our Project Linus family would still be thrilled to attend!

Depending on the year, sometimes I've roomed with Gary and my stepson Marc, another year my parents and still other years with fellow coordinators. This has given me wonderful opportunities to get to know my fellow coordinators. Judie Agee, a dear friend and coordinator from the Phoenix area, was my roomie one year and truly proved to be a godsend. While we were catching up, she confided to me that she had become a private detective. I gave her a task that she completed seamlessly. For years I had been trying to get back in touch with one of my high school best friends, Debi Smoller, but to no avail. I was home a few days from conference and received a call from Judie with a phone number for my long-lost friend. Debi and I reconnected through long phone calls and frequent emails. Within the year, she had passed away from complications of cancer. If it hadn't been for Judie, that door would have probably remained closed forever.

Project Linus continues to make a difference in the lives

of many. As of the end of 2010, our blanket tally exceeded 3.7 million blankets delivered. In 2010 alone, more than 600,000 blankets were delivered! Our mission statement has expanded from "providing security blankets to seriously ill and traumatized children" to "provide love, a sense of security, warmth and comfort to children who are seriously ill, traumatized, or otherwise in need through the gifts of new, handmade blankets and afghans, lovingly created by volunteer Blanketeers." Every day, a new avenue is discovered to complete this mission.

As an Army "brat" and "grand-brat," I spent most of my summers on the D.C. base of Ft. Myer. It is in close proximity to Arlington National Cemetery, where my paternal grandparents, Opa and Oma, are buried. The military has always held a soft spot in my heart. If I had been allowed to become a helicopter pilot, I would have continued my family's tradition. However, during the time I was in college ROTC, women weren't allowed to serve active combat or combat arms roles, so I didn't pursue that vocational path.

During one of our Institute's dinners a few years ago, my parents were moved by a coordinator's story of delivering Project Linus blankets to a military funeral through the Fallen Heroes program. She thought she was going to just drop them off, but when she arrived, she was escorted to the deceased's children. There, she was able to ceremoniously present them with their blankets similar to the tri-cornered flag which was presented to their mother. We have been able to bring comfort to thousands of military children in this way. To me, it seems like the least we can do for someone who gave up his or her life for our country. Marleen Manley, who runs a chapter in the Atlanta area, works closely with the Department of Defense. She contacts coordinators to let them know when a military funeral is scheduled in their area where a deceased child could benefit from receiving a blanket.

Barb "Sprinkles" McLean is not only the coordinator for Northern Idaho and Spokane, Washington, but also the Project Linus hostess for the military effort called TAPS (Tragedy Assistance Program for Survivors). They are America's front-line resource for all who are grieving the death of a loved one who served our country. They provide blankets to children attend a five day Camp Good Grief in the Washington, D.C. area to help them learn lifelong coping skills to get through the loss of a parent. There are mini camps at some individual bases around the country where there have been a large number of service people lost. Project Linus blankets are at these mini camps too.

While she was on Embassy duty in Calcutta, Barb and some co-workers came across a baby whose mother had just passed away in the shadows of the streets. They helped get the mother's body to Mother Teresa's facility called the Home for the Dying so she could receive a proper burial. The little boy was given to Mother Teresa who quickly had assistants retrieve a blanket to bundle the baby. Barb remembers that the blanket was so used that it had patches on its patches. Mother Teresa told her that the little boy would be taken care of, schooled and become an asset to the society.

When Barb came across the Reader's Digest article while vacationing in Alaska, she noticed the same quote that she saw at Mother Teresa's facility- "We do not do great things but we do small things with great love." She knew that she wanted to become involved in Project Linus and was awarded a chapter on her birthday in 1999.

She has also become involved with the group Angel Flights which is a non-profit charitable organization of pilots, volunteers and friends. They arrange free air transportation for legitimate, charitable, medically related needs. The Denver chapter has also used Angel Flights services to get urgently needed blankets to the Aspen area for tennis star Andrea Jaeger's The Silver Lining Foundation for Children with Cancer. Barb was on a flight with two pediatric patients whom she presented with Project Linus blankets. The little boy kept asking her if he could really keep his blankets which Barb continue to give an affirmative answer. When they arrived at their destination, the little boy motioned with his finger that he wanted Barb to come down to his level. As she leaned over, he whispered to her, "Are you God's wife?" That little boy's innocent question helps carry Barb through even her toughest days.

Unfortunately, disasters continue to plague our world—wars, earthquakes, tsunamis, hurricanes, tornadoes, floods, fires, crime, etc. Wherever and whenever it is a financial and logistical possibility, Project Linus is there to offer aid. It is such a powerful tool to know that although we can't stop bad things from happening, we can be there to assist with the aftermath.

I'm utterly blissful in my role with Project Linus as Founder, Coordinator and Blanketeer. I am sure that life holds many more exciting opportunities in the future. I continue to appreciate the gift of the *Oprah* experience. To this day, I use my "Thank You" mug whenever I want an extra reminder that amazing things are possible.

Acknowledgments

They say it takes a village to raise a child. It also seemed to take a village to write this book. To highlight just a few standouts that have particularly helped bring this book to fruition, I would like to thank the following:

Andrea Costantine, Donna Mazzitelli, and Tina Taylor – who truly made this book come alive from my computer to the book you are holding in your hands. The three best book midwives a writer could have!

Fellow writers who patiently allowed me to extract from their own learning's from their book writing adventures- Diane Beil, Monique Stauder, Dan and Manon Rodriquez, Eric Reamer, Angel Tuccy, Polly Letofsky, Parker Creative

Writers Social Club and the Parker Writers Group.

My patient proofreaders – Tonya Gray, Jeaneane Childers, Diane Beal, France Komoroske and Kevin Crossley who weren't afraid to point out areas of improvement in a kind and constructive manner.

My Project Linus Family from Headquarters to Coordinators to Blanketeers to recipients and their families who graciously shared stories.

My Southeast Denver chapter has been blessed by so many helpful hands. Betsy Elliott continues to walk on water. Sue Kroepsch now has the unenviable task of keeping me focused. She is the liaison with the local chapter of Denver Community Knitting Group who meet monthly at the Parker Library and keep us well supplied with beautifully knitted and crocheted blankets. Sue helps locate recipient facilities and is instrumental in deliveries. Alice Dice is my quilter who can be counted on to jump to the rescue when we need emergency quilts and help with foreign country deliveries. Emi Duke, Laurie Schneyer and the Prairie Stitchers from Prairie Unitarian Universalist Church for label sewing and moral support.

An additional shout out to Diane Beil who has been there for my chapter and me every step of the way over the past decade. Her daughter, Keleigh, is a two time Project Linus blanket recipient (received a second after their house burned to the foundation along with all of their belongings). This mother-daughter duo regularly assists with blanket day events, sews labels in their home, and Keleigh is one of our most effective speakers. Diane leads by example- conduce per examplem!

My Fabulous Four – loyal friends who have stuck with

me for decades – Tina Taylor, graphic artist extraordinaire, Tammy Rafferty, blanket pick up person and sounding board especially on our hikes, Jill Malcolm who was a coordinator in Maryland and Ken Manson who has been a compassionate ear and financial supporter of Project Linus.

Lunch Out Loud Toastmasters for being an open stage for Project Linus tales and an empathetic home for honing speaking and leadership skills.

Music has always held a strong key to my heart. Some of my favorite musicians have been quoted in the book. When I was having trouble finding appropriate titles for certain chapters, I resorted to one of my all time favorites- Sting's- song titles. In fact, there are twelve from him. Some are quite popular, others I was surprised to see including "Peanuts" for Chapter 17.

Charles Schulz for the inspiration of Linus and United Media for lending the image to our effort.

My family – parents Charles and Valerie for instilling in me at an early age the need to give back to the community. My brother Glenn, his wife Laurie and kiddos Miriam and Charlie for being my cheerleaders. My parent in laws – Don and Lil Rinedollar for giving me such a perfect life partner and being so encouraging along with my sister-in-laws Chris and Vicky. My cousin Marily and her beautiful daughter Tsehaynesh, who graces the book's back cover.

Gary, my husband- blanket maker and schlepper, corporate relations guru and all around Mr. Wonderful. He has been so patient and supportive through the book writing process as well as life in general. I count my lucky stars everyday for him being who he is. Lastly, The Higher Power, that makes all things possible. I am truly Living the Dream!

About the Author

Karen Loucks Rinedollar was a child of the 60's and learned at an early age to question authority. As an Army brat and grandbrat, Karen appreciates the freedoms that the U.S. affords its citizens and conversely believes in the theory- Give Peace a Chance!

Always one to champion the innocent, especially children and animals, she was moved to action when spotting an image of a child with cancer in a 1995 Parade magazine article. With a Herculean response to solve a need to comfort seriously ill and traumatized children, she founded Project Linus. Within months, the word about this handmade security blanket effort had reached both coasts and quickly traversed its way across the middle of the country and around the world. To date, millions of these blankets have found their way into the hands and homes of the world's children.

Karen never takes a single day for granted. This allows her to live powerfully with passion and purpose, without fear of failure. She is known to fit more into a day than many would fit into a week. Her mother described her in People magazine as having two speeds- fast and faster! Karen has the need for speed and action.

She has been called a "serial entrepreneur" – seeing opportunity in all facets of life. This first time author, is also a Wedding Officiant, Invoice Discounter, co-owner of Boulder's Roundhouse Spirits distillery, is a Toastmaster, is on the Board of Directors for the Parker Chamber of Commerce, Chairperson of Colorado's Resource for Events and Weddings, continues to volunteer for Rattlesnake Fire as a Community Relations Specialist and is the Project Linus coordinator for Southeast Denver.

In her spare time, she enjoys travel, reading nonfiction and the joys of her beloved garden with fresh produce, colorful flowers and a pumpkin patch that would make Linus smile.

She is married to the love of her life Gary, aka Mr. Wonderful. Two step-kids, Kristen and Marcus, goldfish and Zuma the cat complete the family package.

Karen is available for keynote presentations, personal appearances and wedding officiating. To contact her:

KarenRinedollar@aol.com

www.workingforpeanuts.org

www.facebook.com/ProjectLinusWorkingforPeanuts

A percentage of the proceeds from this book will be
donated to Project Linus.

Made in the USA
Charleston, SC
28 July 2011